Roger Olson's *Against Liberal Theology*  definition, examination, and evaluatic tic, orthodox Christian theology in the one liberal (not progressive) theologian after another. In their own words, Olson often shines a bright, piercing light on their own criticisms. This is a vintage example of Olson being Olson: he knows the literature, he is candid, he is fair, and he is unstinting in criticism of the pitfalls of liberal theologians. And he examines only those who overtly espouse "liberal" in their theology. Those most attracted into progressivism and then into liberalism will benefit from a humble reading of this book.

—**Scot McKnight,** professor of New
Testament, Northern Seminary

Roger Olson shows us the absolute theological vacuity of American liberal Christianity. He demonstrates that liberalism's God is a mirror of themselves, their Jesus is not worthy of worship nor a savior of any sort, and the Holy Spirit is merely a symbol for their own musings. Olson's verdict is damning but indubitable: liberal Christianity has little to do with classic or historical Christianity.

—**Michael Bird,** academic dean and lecturer
in New Testament, Ridley College

AGAINST
LIBERAL
THEOLOGY

AGAINST
LIBERAL
THEOLOGY

PUTTING THE BRAKES ON
PROGRESSIVE CHRISTIANITY

ROGER E. OLSON

ZONDERVAN
REFLECTIVE

ZONDERVAN REFLECTIVE

Against Liberal Theology
Copyright © 2022 by Roger E. Olson

Requests for information should be addressed to:
Zondervan, *3900 Sparks Dr. SE, Grand Rapids, Michigan 49546*

Zondervan titles may be purchased in bulk for educational, business, fundraising, or sales promotional use. For information, please email SpecialMarkets@Zondervan.com.

ISBN 978-0-310-13943-0 (softcover)
ISBN 978-0-310-13946-1 (audio)
ISBN 978-0-310-13944-7 (ebook)

Cover design: Micah Kandros Design
Cover photo: © Kyle Lundquist / Shutterstock
Interior design: Sara Colley

Printed in the United States of America

22 23 24 25 26 27 28 29 30 /TRM/ 12 11 10 9 8 7 6 5 4 3 2 1

CONTENTS

PREFACE

In today's culture it is not popular to be against something unless it's blatantly immoral or illegal. Even then, the question often arises about moral issues: who are you to be against something that doesn't hurt anyone? So we feel the pressure not to be against people's beliefs. And yet, as a Christian theologian, I do not see how we can escape it. I can't be for everything that goes under the label Christian. And some things people call Christian just can't be if the Bible and Christian history are our guides. It really is that simple. I am well aware how unpopular that is to say, but anyone who knows just how diverse *Christianity* is as a label has to know that not everything called by it can be authentically Christian. Anything that is compatible with everything is nothing. If *Christianity* is to mean something, it has to have some shape, if not boundaries.

I apologize to anyone who feels hurt by my being against liberal Christianity. Hurting anyone's feelings is not my aim. Rather, my aim is to inform people what liberal Christianity is and why they ought to think critically about it. If they choose to embrace it anyway, that's not something I can or want to prevent. But I want people to know what they are embracing and why it is controversial and almost certainly not their best option insofar as they want to be authentically Christian.

Someone once said that the only thing wrong with process theology—a popular form of liberal Christianity—is that it is such an attractive alternative to Christian faith. I know it sounds harsh, but at least that person acknowledged, rightly, that process theology is attractive. I will say the same about liberal Christianity: it is attractive in some ways and to many people. But I must add that, properly understood (and explaining it properly is a major goal here), it is an alternative to true, classical, historical, biblical, and orthodox Christianity.

For years I have taught my theology students to live by the motto "Before saying 'I disagree,' be sure you can say 'I understand.'" I have spent years studying and even "trying on" liberal Christianity. I have studied it and taught about it in classes. I have organized and participated in liberal-evangelical dialogue events. I have invited self-identified liberal pastors and theologians to speak to my classes. I have read more books of liberal Christianity than I can count and have been a member of two liberal churches: one Presbyterian and one Baptist. I have attended conferences and retreats and symposia of liberal theological scholars. I have studied under liberal biblical scholars and theologians during my graduate studies. I do not come against liberal Christianity as an outsider; I know it and understand it and have experienced it as an insider, even though I have always maintained my own warmhearted evangelical Christian faith and orthodox theology.

So why write a book like this one—*against* liberal Christianity? Many people, including many liberal theologians, admit that classical liberal Protestantism has been declining in popularity for decades. That may be, but I have seen many conservative Christian young people (and some older people) abandon their orthodox Christian faith in favor of liberal Christianity, most often, in my experience, in reaction against what they perceive as the fundamentalism of their Christian nurture. They grew up in fundamentalist churches, found them stifling, anti-intellectual, legalistic, whatever, and rushed past the middle ground to the opposite end of the Christian spectrum, to liberal Christianity. And I have observed that, in many cases, these "converts" to liberal Christianity never stopped to think about its flaws. I want to warn Christians against uncritically embracing liberal Christianity, and I want to encourage those who find themselves in liberal churches either to work to change it—back toward warmhearted and biblical, orthodox Christianity—or to leave it.

■ ■ ■

I want to thank my teaching and research assistant Collin Glatz for his invaluable help with feedback on this book's manuscript. I also want to thank my Zondervan editor Matthew Estel for his constructive criticisms and helpful corrections.

I dedicate this book to my friends of a lifetime Greg H. and Galen Paul F.

INTRODUCTION

Theology, in the sense meant here, is a set of beliefs about God and things related to God. Christianity, in the sense meant here, is the believing of those beliefs. This book is about both, and its focus is a particular tradition of beliefs and the believing of those beliefs. Liberal theology is a modern tradition of beliefs; liberal Christianity is the modern way of believing those beliefs. This book is a warning aimed mainly at those who think of themselves as progressive Christians—to not adopt liberal theology or believe in the liberal Christian way. Many regard progressive Christianity as a path toward liberal theology and Christianity; there is some truth in that.

This book, however, is not a diatribe against progressive Christianity. *Progressive* is a label used by many different kinds of Christians. I do wish to warn at least some who identify as progressive Christians against sliding into liberal Christianity. Of course, these labels are complicated because some truly liberal Christians—as I will describe them here—prefer to call themselves progressive Christians. But many who call themselves progressive Christians are not really liberal in the sense

I mean it in this book (and I will explain that in great detail). So, to put this simply, not all progressive Christians are liberal Christians, even if all liberal Christians at least sometimes call themselves progressive Christians.

So why am I not writing against progressive Christianity? For one thing, unlike liberal Christianity, there is no tradition of progressive Christianity, nor was there ever a cohesive movement of progressive Christians. *Progressive Christian* is far too flexible to pin down. Some very conservative Protestants have called their theology progressive dispensationalism.[1] During the 1970s a group of evangelical Christians developed a style and coalition that has come to be called progressive evangelicals.[2] By no means does *progressive* necessarily point to the same type of theology as *liberal*. This book is really only about true liberal Christianity and its theology; toward the end I will issue a warning to *some* Christians who call themselves progressive about not sliding into true liberal Christianity, something that does often happen but for which there is no necessity.

Liberal Christianity constitutes a tradition that grew out of a movement. It is not monolithic or homogeneous. It is a diverse tradition with some common, unifying features. In this book, I will focus mainly on its common features as a somewhat unified tradition within modern Christianity. Many books have been published describing it that way. I will mention one magisterial set of books by a single author

---

1. See Craig Alan Blaising and Darrell Bock, *Progressive Dispensationalism* (Grand Rapids: Baker, 1993).

2. See Brantley W. Gasaway, *Progressive Evangelicals and the Pursuit of Social Justice* (Chapel Hill, NC: Univ. of North Carolina Press, 2014), and David R. Swartz, *Moral Minority: The Evangelical Left in an Age of Conservatism* (Philadelphia: Univ. of Pennsylvania Press, 2012).

and two one-volume treatments of the tradition. All of these focus primarily on American liberal Christianity and especially its distinctive theology. Liberal Christianity actually began in Germany with a pastor-theologian named Friedrich Schleiermacher (1768–1834), and it found its most important prototype, influencer, in a later German theologian named Albrecht Ritschl (1822–89). Numerous American pastors and theologians flocked to Germany to study with these men, and most of them returned to America to "modernize" American Christianity with ideas borrowed from them and later German liberal theologians such as Adolf von Harnack (1851–1930) and Ernst Troeltsch (1865–1923).

The focus here, however, will be on American liberal Christianity, which owes a great debt to those German pioneers of liberal theology. Some mention of them will appear here, but not to worry—no knowledge of theology is assumed in this book. You, the reader, will not be overwhelmed with technical theological jargon or required to know and understand philosophies that influenced liberal Christianity (although some mention of them must be made). This book intends to be user friendly even as it asks readers to think about matters they may not have encountered previously or thought about deeply.

American liberal Christianity, including its background in German (and English) liberal theologies, is described, examined, analyzed, and evaluated in a three-volume work by Union Theological Seminary professor Gary Dorrien (b. 1952). Its title is *The Making of American Liberal Theology.*[3] The set

---

3. Gary J. Dorrien, *The Making of American Liberal Theology*, 3 vols. (Louisville: Westminster John Knox, 2001–6).

encompasses well over a thousand pages and describes in great detail dozens of influential American liberal Christian thinkers and leaders. Two other important and influential books of the same genre are *The Impact of American Religious Liberalism* by Kenneth Cauthen and *The Modernist Impulse in American Protestantism* by William R. Hutchinson.[4] In this book, I will use material from these three histories of American liberal Christianity as well as many other sources mostly by American liberal theologians, pastors, teachers, and laypeople. For the most part I will avoid relying on polemical works against liberal Christianity, especially ones that do not display objective knowledge of the subject.

Again, I wish to emphasize that I have no ax to grind with liberal Christians; I do not hate them but love them. I just think their theology is seriously flawed to the extent that true liberal Christianity ought not to be considered authentically Christian. Honesty calls for liberal Christians to admit that they have "cut the cord of continuity" between their religion and historical, classical, orthodox Christianity to the extent that their religion is a different one.

I will not argue that liberal Christians are not Christians; I will argue that their theology is not authentically Christian. Insofar as Christianity is a matter of the heart rather than the head, liberal Christians may be authentically Christian. It is their theology that comes under critical scrutiny here, and my opinion, based on many years of studying liberal

---

4. Kenneth Cauthen, *The Impact of American Religious Liberalism*, 2nd ed. (1962; Lanham, MD: Univ. Press of America, 1983), and William R. Hutchinson, *The Modernist Impulse in American Protestantism* (1976; New York and Oxford: Oxford Univ. Press, 1982).

Christianity, is that liberal theology is not authentically Christian because it departs so radically from biblical and traditional Christian orthodoxy.

This argument was made almost a century ago by an earlier critic of liberal Christianity named J. Gresham Machen (1881–1937) in his book *Christianity and Liberalism*.[5] However, Machen assumed a much narrower vision of orthodox Christianity than I have. I fear that he might even have considered *me* a liberal Christian! Machen was an early fundamentalist who counted the substitutionary atonement—that on the cross Jesus suffered the wrath of God in our place—an essential doctrine of classical, orthodox Christianity. My vision of "mere Christianity" looks to what all Christians everywhere have always believed—which is called the Vincentian Canon. It is transdenominational and very basic. It is something like what is called *Basic Christianity* in the book of that title written by English pastor-theologian John Stott (1921–2011).[6]

Machen understood liberal Christianity well. He studied in Germany under liberal theologian Wilhelm Herrmann (1846–1922) and was no slouch when it came to knowing, understanding, and correctly describing liberal Christianity. He concluded that it is so different from classical, historical, orthodox Christianity that it should not be considered Christian. It is, he argued, a different religion even if it uses much of the same language as Christianity. One thing that made Machen's book so famous and influential is that a leading secular humanist of that time, commentator Walter Lippmann (1889–1974), publicly agreed with Machen that

---

5. J. Gresham Machen, *Christianity and Liberalism* (New York: Macmillan, 1923).
6. John Stott, *Basic Christianity* (Downers Grove, IL: InterVarsity Press, 1958).

liberal Christianity is not real Christianity and that liberal Christians should give up the label *Christian* and call their religion something else.

This book is not just a repeat of Machen's book, although its conclusion will be similar. A great deal has changed within the liberal Christian tradition since 1923, and this book will take some of those changes into account. They are not necessarily changes for the better, although in at least one case a change within the tradition moved it back closer to orthodox Christianity. That change was the reintroduction of *a* doctrine of universal sinfulness, a doctrine largely lost in the older liberal Christianity of Machen's time.

I am crucially, even somewhat nervously, aware that some potential readers of this book may be hesitating because I have not yet defined what *I* mean by liberal Christianity. A full description of that has to wait; it will take time. However, for the sake of those considering whether to buy and read this book, I realize I must here and now give at least a foretaste of what is to come.

The generally agreed-on definition of liberal Christianity, liberal theology, is "maximal acknowledgment of the claims of modernity in Christian thinking about doctrines." This widely accepted, extremely brief definition was given by historical theologian Claude Welch in his magisterial *Protestant Thought in the Nineteenth Century*.[7] Modernity is the cultural mindset stemming from the Enlightenment and scientific revolutions of the seventeenth and eighteenth centuries. Generally speaking, compared with previous Western cultures, and contrary

---

7. Claude Welch, *Protestant Thought in the Nineteenth Century* (New Haven, CT: Yale Univ. Press, 1972, 1985).

to many non-Western cultures, modernity breathes a secular or at least nonsupernatural spirit. It places great faith in the scientific method, in reason, and in the right and responsibility of every individual to think for himself or herself. It inclines against anything supernatural, including miracles, often seeing them as superstition.

"Maximal acknowledgment of the claims of modernity" does not mean total agreement with everything modern thinkers say. It means that liberal Christians *tend* to reinterpret Scripture, doctrine, thought, and religious experience in terms of modernity, giving modern thought authority alongside, if not over, Scripture and tradition. In most cases that means a nonsupernatural interpretation of the Bible and Christianity—a Christianity without miracles.

Gary Dorrien defines liberal Christianity as Christianity that recognizes no authority outside the self. German philosopher Immanuel Kant wrote an essay titled "What Is Enlightenment?" (1784) in which he defined it as "thinking for yourself." Dorrien seems to pick up on that and use it as part of a definition and description of liberal Christianity. Liberal Christianity, for him, is Christianity based primarily on the individual's religious experience and experiences of culture without acceptance of any external authority, including Scripture and tradition.[8] Most liberal Christians, however, would add to Dorrien's definition that one ought to pay heed to universal human religious experience even if the ultimate authority for deciding what is true lies within the individual. In most cases, this means a Christianity that has "moved out

---

8. Gary J. Dorrien, *The Making of American Liberal Theology: Idealism, Realism, and Modernity, 1900–1950* (Louisville: Westminster John Knox, 2003), xiii.

of the 'house of authority.'" The authority of the Bible and of tradition is subsumed under the authority of individual reason, experience, and conscience.

John Wesley scholar Albert Outler (1908–89) described Wesley's theological method using the rubric of a "Wesleyan Quadrilateral" of Scripture, tradition, reason, and experience. In Wesley's scheme, Scripture has primacy over tradition, while reason and experience are used as tools of interpretation.[9] Liberal Christians tend to begin the theological search for truth and conversation with reason and experience and then draw upon Scripture as "our sacred stories" and Christian tradition as simply the history of Christian interpretation of Scripture and Christian experience. Conservative Christians would begin with Scripture as the supreme authority over all and draw on tradition to fill in the gaps and help interpret Scripture while respecting the use of reason and experience as tools of interpretation without authority.

It would be helpful now to allow a liberal Christian theologian to express what liberal Christian theology means, especially in terms of its deep, underlying difference from conservative, orthodox Christian theology. Our guide is liberal Christian theologian Delwin Brown (b. 1935), who began teaching Christian theology in a conservative Christian university and seminary but ended his career teaching in a liberal Methodist seminary. According to him, "Liberalism [in theology] holds that a view of God must in each age be reevaluated and reconceived in light of our best views about the world. The Christian concept of God must cohere with the rest of modern

---

9. For a detailed analysis of this Wesleyan Quadrilateral, see Donald Thorsen, *The Wesleyan Quadrilateral: An Introduction* (Lexington: Emeth, 2005).

knowledge."[10] Also, "Liberalism at its best is . . . likely to say 'We certainly ought to honor the richness of our Christian past and appreciate the vast contribution it makes to our lives, finally we must live by our best modern conclusions . . . our commitment, however tentative and self-critically maintained, must be to the careful judgments of the present age, even if they differ radically from the dictates of the past.'"[11] Whenever there is a perceived conflict between the Bible and/ or Christian tradition, on the one hand, and the "best of modern thought," on the other hand, the latter trumps the former. This is a respectable, honest, and forthright admission on the part of a mainstream liberal Christian theologian.

As we will see throughout this book, however, the issue becomes what "the best of modern thought" entails. Even most conservative Christian scholars and theologians freely and gladly correlate and integrate all truth, saying there can really be no conflict between revealed truth in the Bible and "true truth" outside the Bible. But what if the best of modern thought is only a passing fashion of thought, a philosophy of the moment, a cultural fad? Is not postmodernity teaching us that much that was considered "settled truth" in modern thought is now questionable? This question will haunt liberal Christianity throughout this book. Could it be that by adjusting and accommodating Christianity to whatever culture requires, one is sacrificing the prophetic power of Christianity on the altar of respectability?

Most liberal Christians are not theologians and may rebel

10. Clark H. Pinnock and Delwin Brown, *Theological Crossfire: An Evangelical/ Liberal Dialogue* (Grand Rapids: Zondervan, 1990), 82–83.
11. Ibid., 23.

against the emphasis on theologians throughout this book. The problem is, of course, that it is the theologians of liberal Christianity who generally set the agenda for liberal Christians. Their ideas trickle down and ripple out into churches and affect the beliefs and lives of "ordinary Christians"—those who never attend seminary or write theology books or pastor churches. Many of these people do not buy into liberal Christianity entirely but are nevertheless led by it, directly or indirectly, into a path of Christian thinking and living that is subject to the weaknesses and flaws of liberal theology pointed out in this book. They will have to decide to what degree the shoe fits them, the shoe being the theological ideas about Christianity expressed by liberal theologians such as Brown.

Some readers may wonder how liberal Christianity still exists and is worth writing against if postmodernity is replacing modernity. Isn't "the best of *modern* thought" part of the definition of liberal theology? Whatever postmodernity is or becomes (which is still being worked out), liberal Christianity will inevitably adjust and accommodate Christianity to the best of postmodern thought, because what Brown and other liberal theologians really meant (and mean) is that liberal theology looks to the best of *contemporary* culture and thought as authoritative for Christian theology. That doesn't mean "contemporary worship" or even just "trying to be relevant to contemporary people." Yet whatever is viewed as the best of contemporary culture and thought, whether modern or postmodern, becomes the supreme norm for liberal Christianity, especially in terms of working out its beliefs, its teachings, its focus, its mission.

So what's wrong with liberal Christianity? Well, that will

be the focus of this book—to demonstrate why true liberal Christianity is inimical, even pernicious, to true Christianity. For example, to preview one part of the argument, by and large, liberal Christianity reduces Jesus Christ to a mere man who revealed God to people but who was not himself God. This view is sometimes called functional Christology because it claims that Jesus Christ only functioned as God but was not actually God. That is an enormous departure from classical, historical, biblical, orthodox Christianity. It cuts the cord of continuity with the Bible and with ancient and Reformation Christianity. Even the ecumenical World Council of Churches requires member denominations to affirm that "Jesus Christ is God and Savior." Liberal Christians may struggle to say complimentary things about Jesus Christ as, for example, the "human face of God," but in the end they often cannot bring themselves to affirm that he was ontologically—in his very being—God incarnate. The liberal ways of expressing the uniqueness of Jesus Christ reduce him to a man different in degree but not different in kind from other great religious wise men and prophets. That opens the door wide to religious pluralism—the belief that there are many saviors and lords, Jesus Christ being one of them. That is a deep betrayal of true Christianity.

Many more problems with liberal Christianity are brought to light throughout this book. All kinds of religious groups call themselves Christian and teach ideas and practices absolutely contrary to anything known as Christian for many centuries going back to the New Testament itself. At some point liberal Christianity stepped over the line into unchristian territory, just as have numerous cults and sects throughout the centuries. If Christianity is compatible with anything and everything, it is nothing.

The story of liberal Christianity really begins with a group known as the Unitarians. The whole story, or as much of it as can be told in such a brief book, will have to wait for the chapter about the history of liberal Christianity, but a brief introduction is in order. Sometime in the late eighteenth century, a group of men and women in England and then in New England formed new churches based on allegedly enlightened ideas about religion, including Christianity. They called their movement Unitarianism, and many Congregational and some Baptist churches joined the fledgling denomination. By the 1820s the movement had become culturally significant. Several American presidents, beginning with John Quincy Adams (president 1825–29), have been Unitarians. The first Unitarians considered themselves Christians but did not believe in the Trinity, the deity of Jesus Christ, or hell. Eventually another religious group called the Universalists joined with the Unitarians, and the denomination came to be known as the Unitarian-Universalist Fellowship of Churches, which still exists today. Now, however, it is not distinctively Christian. The first Unitarians considered themselves Christians but acknowledged their radical differences from traditional Christian orthodoxy. Eventually many did begin to acknowledge that they were not Christians. That was honest of them.

What is the point of that story about the Unitarians? Most liberal Christians who remained outside the Unitarian movement, within so-called mainline Protestant churches, came to believe much like the original Unitarians. Mainline

Protestantism changed to allow essentially Unitarian beliefs (or unbeliefs) to thrive within their churches and seminaries. Of course, liberal Christianity evolved far beyond its beginnings with the Unitarians of the late seventeenth and early eighteenth centuries. Still, and nevertheless, many liberal Christians in mainline churches have given up their beliefs in the deity of Jesus Christ, the Trinity, miracles, and hell. The main difference is that they did not and do not call themselves Unitarians. In a strange way, early Unitarianism was born and raised, in terms of its theology, within mainline Protestantism in Europe and America, only disguising itself as authentically Christian. Many Americans, and many others, would look at the beliefs of the Unitarian-Universalist church and say, "Well, those are nice folks, but they aren't Christians." But the same people do not notice that the same basic theology exists in their own mainline Protestant churches. The theologians and leaders of liberal Christianity ought to be honest and proclaim themselves Unitarians rather than Christians.

That sounds harsh, but so did the pronouncements of the Old Testament prophets about Israel's idolatries. So did the criticisms of Jesus aimed at the people who controlled the centers of Jewish religion in his time. So did the apostles' and early church fathers' verbal attacks on false Christians within the primitive and ancient churches. Certainly the Gnostics who denied the bodily resurrection got defensive when the apostles and church fathers pronounced them heretics. Second-century bishop Irenaeus (c. 130–c. 202) wrote five books *Against Heresies*, and he is celebrated for it because the heresies he exposed as not truly Christian are now generally recognized as false. But what about today? What would Irenaeus or other church fathers, to say nothing of the apostles, say about liberal Christianity? I am convinced they would say "heresy!"

Throughout this book my main argument will be that liberal Christianity cuts the cord of continuity between itself and biblical, historical, classical, orthodox Christianity so thoroughly that it ought to call itself something other than Christian. Biblical, historical, classical, orthodox Christianity is expressed in the creeds accepted as definitive for true Christianity by Christians of all major traditions: Eastern Orthodox, Roman Catholic, traditional Protestant, and even the "radical Reformation" and "free" churches. The truths expressed in the Apostles' Creed and the Nicene Creed have been warmly embraced and taught even in Protestant churches that call themselves noncreedal.

Before going further, I want to make absolutely clear that, at least for me, here, *liberal* does not apply to political beliefs or commitments. When I write here about liberalism and liberals, I mean only theological liberalism and liberal theologians. This book is not about politics, economics, social philosophies, or mere open-mindedness to new ideas (to say nothing of liberality toward the poor). In this book, the subject is only liberal theology as taught by men and women who claim to speak and write as Christians. The subject is doctrines and teachings of intellectuals and preachers who claim to be Christians but cannot really be Christians intellectually—in terms of their theology. As I will demonstrate, they have cut the cord of continuity so radically that what they teach as modern Christianity is counterfeit Christianity, a false gospel, apostasy.

All the theologians I use to represent liberal Christian

theology claim to be liberal theologically and have written about liberal Christian theology. They are all noted representatives of that tradition, all gladly accept the label *liberal* for their theological orientations, and all are widely recognized as prototypical representatives of liberal Christian theology. They are a diverse group and yet have much in common, including their basic approach to authority in theology, the nature of theology itself, the nature of God and of Jesus Christ, the meaning of salvation, the nonreality of miracles, and the authority of modernity, the culture of the Enlightenment, and (allegedly) modern science.

CHAPTER 1

THE LIBERAL CHRISTIAN TRADITION AND ITS THEOLOGY

In this chapter, I will be writing about preachers and theologians who considered (and consider) themselves Christians, but whom I cannot consider authentically Christian because of their radical departures from traditional, biblical, orthodox Christianity. I will simply call them liberals, liberal theologians, or liberal Christians. Occasionally, I will mention one or two (or a few) who are widely considered liberals theologically whom I do not consider to be such.

For example, in his magisterial three-volume set *The Making of Liberal Theology: Imagining Progressive Religion*, Gary Dorrien includes as a liberal Christian theologian American pastor Horace Bushnell (1802–76). Dorrien devotes one of his longest chapters to that New England Congregational pastor and theologian. I have studied and written about Bushnell and do not consider him truly liberal theologically; I consider him a genuine Christian and the main proponent of progressive orthodoxy, which is not liberal theology. Bushnell presented in his writings and sermons some new interpretations of orthodox doctrines, but he did not cut the cord of continuity between his own theology and historical, classical, Christian orthodoxy. Dorrien admits Bushnell's orthodoxy but includes him in *The Making of Liberal Theology* because his disciples went much further in reinterpreting Christianity and became liberal theologically. Bushnell is for me a good example of a Christian whose theology was progressive but not liberal.

So who are the prototypes of liberal Christian theology? And how did liberal Christian theology begin and progress? The first true liberal theologian, the founder of liberal Christianity, the main prototype of the tradition, was Friedrich Schleiermacher (1768–1834), a German pastor, educator, public intellectual, and theologian. He is almost universally regarded as the founder of liberal theology. There were liberal thinkers who considered themselves Christians before Schleiermacher, but he was a "Prince of the Church," to borrow the title of a book by theologian Brian Gerrish of the University of Chicago Divinity School.[1] Liberal Christian thinkers before Schleiermacher were not churchmen, pastors, or theologians in the same way as he. Before Schleiermacher, many of the

---

1. Brian Gerrish, *A Prince of the Church: Friedrich Schleiermacher and the Beginnings of Modern Theology* (Eugene, OR: Wipf and Stock, 2001). This book consists of the published Rockwell Lectures given at Rice University when I was a student there; I heard these lectures-chapters and then read the book. It is the best brief introduction to Schleiermacher and his theology. However, I have read numerous books by and about Schleiermacher, lectured about Schleiermacher's theology, and written chapters about it in *Twentieth-Century Theology: God and the World in a Transitional Age*, coauthored with Stanley J. Grenz (Downers Grove, IL: InterVarsity Press, 1992), and in *The Journey of Modern Theology: From Reconstruction to Deconstruction* (Downers Grove, IL: InterVarsity Press, 1999).

same ideas were believed and taught by deists and Unitarians, for example. But Schleiermacher was a leading minister of the Prussian Union Church, the state church of Prussia—a hybrid of Reformed and Lutheran.

Something new appeared with Schleiermacher. With Schleiermacher liberal Christianity was born. But what he birthed was a new species, not authentic Christianity. Later liberals stand on Schleiermacher's shoulders or, to change metaphors, follow in the path he carved out. Those who followed him have not all agreed about the details, but they have all agreed with his basic approach, expressing Christianity in a modern idiom.

Schleiermacher was raised in a pietist Christian home, attended a pietist church, and went to a pietist university, but he radically diverged from that tradition, much to his father's dismay. The pietists were orthodox Christians who emphasized personal conversion, being "born again," and having a personal relationship with Jesus Christ.[2] Pietists were and are evangelical Christians who combine biblical-orthodox Christian belief with warmhearted Christian spirituality. To his father, who expressed strong disappointment with his son's new ideas about Christianity, Schleiermacher wrote (in a letter) that he was still a pietist but "of a higher order."[3]

Schleiermacher was concerned that many of the educated, cultured elites of Berlin, where he lived, thought that being religious and especially Christian conflicted with being

---

2. For more about pietism, see Roger E. Olson and Christian T. Collins Winn, *Reclaiming Pietism: Retrieving an Evangelical Tradition* (Grand Rapids: Eerdmans, 2015).

3. James C. Livingston, *The Enlightenment and the Nineteenth Century*, vol. 1 of *Modern Christian Thought*, 2nd ed. (Upper Saddle River, NJ: Prentice Hall, 1997), 94.

enlightened, modern, and sophisticated (in the truest and best sense). To them he wrote a massive apologetic for religion titled *On Religion: Speeches to Its Cultured Despisers* (1799). There he argued that religion is "God-consciousness," and everyone has some degree of that "feeling of utter dependence on God." He equated religion with God-consciousness. Later he wrote a massive systematic theology titled *The Christian Faith* (1830), in which he expressed liberal theology, radically transforming Christianity from orthodoxy into a form acceptable to modern, enlightened people. For example, he defined Jesus Christ as the fully God-conscious man and denied his ontological deity, his preexistence, and his incarnation. He also denied Jesus' bodily resurrection, miracles, and second coming in the future. The foundational source for his theology was first and foremost the Christian experience of Jesus Christ as redeemer through the church, Jesus' communication of his own God-consciousness to Christians.

Nobody with any deep acquaintance with Schleiermacher would doubt his spirituality, his profound religious nature, his enthusiasm for Jesus Christ as a living person, or his love for God and the church. However, nobody with any deep acquaintance with his theology could doubt that he broke the cord of continuity between his doctrinal formulations and orthodoxy. He relegated the Trinity to an appendix to *The Christian Faith* and expressed it as three modes of God-consciousness rather than as three distinct persons of the eternal Godhead. As mentioned earlier, there were precursors of liberal theology before him, but Schleiermacher almost singlehandedly founded the new tradition known as liberal theology.

Fast-forward two hundred years to contemporary liberal

theologian Douglas Ottati, an American Presbyterian theologian and author of several books, including the massive systematic theology *A Theology for the Twenty-First Century* (2020).[4] Although there are significant differences in details and expressions, Ottati's theology continues the basic tradition of Schleiermacher. Anyone who reads Schleiermacher's *The Christian Faith* and then reads Ottati's *A Theology for the Twenty-First Century* cannot miss the similarities. For example, Ottati labels Jesus Christ the God-filled man, meaning Jesus had the paradigmatic *human* experience of God. Also like Schleiermacher, Ottati relegates the Trinity to an appendix and describes the three persons of the Trinity as three *ways* Christians experience God. Schleiermacher and Ottati, almost two centuries apart, treat Christian experience of God as the primary source and norm of Christian theology and doctrine. And both permit what they understand to be the best of modern culture, especially philosophy and the sciences, to determine what enlightened Christians can believe.

Between Schleiermacher and Ottati stands a host of liberal theologians who considered themselves modern Christians and who are widely considered to be great Christian thinkers and influencers. What stands out about all of them is their commitment to reconstructing Christian beliefs in terms of modernity, the largely secular Western zeitgeist ("spirit of the age") growing out of the Enlightenment and the scientific revolution. Before describing some of the leading liberal thinkers and their unique contributions to liberal theology, it will be helpful to expound some major

---

4. Douglas F. Ottati, *A Theology for the Twenty-First Century* (Grand Rapids: Eerdmans, 2020).

scholarly opinions about the liberal theological tradition stemming from Schleiermacher.

Gary Dorrien is by far the most astute and highly regarded historian of the liberal Christian tradition. Dorrien says, "Liberal Christian thinkers have argued that religion should be interpreted from the standpoint of modern knowledge and experience."[5] He emphasizes liberal theology's rejection of external authority and its reliance on the authority of the self—even in religion, even in Christianity. According to Dorrien, although there have been and are varieties of liberal Christianity and liberal theology, something holds them together as one tradition:

> One way or another, liberal theology always took its stand on the verdicts of modern knowledge and experience without bowing to external authority claims. . . . [Liberal theologians] accepted the naturalistic premises of modern historiography and the modernist valorization of objective knowledge. They specialized in cultural accommodation and religious progressivism. Every liberal theologian sought to bring Christian claims into line with beliefs derived from modern critical consciousness, and thus . . . took for granted that the authority of reason makes the mythical aspects of Christianity problematic for modern theology.[6]

---

5. Gary J. Dorrien, *The Making of American Liberal Theology: Imagining Progressive Religion, 1805–1900* (Louisville: Westminster John Knox, 2001), xiii. This is the first of the three volumes; each has its own title after the general title of *The Making of American Liberal Theology*.

6. Gary J. Dorrien, *The Making of American Liberal Theology: Idealism, Realism, and Modernity, 1900–1950* (Louisville: Westminster John Knox, 2003), 534.

Dorrien adds, "All American liberal theology has been modernist . . . which refers to the displacement of gospel norms by a modern worldview."[7]

What "gospel norms" and what "mythical aspects of Christianity" has liberal theology considered problematic and displaced (or replaced)? As I will show in the doctrinal chapters (beginning with chapter 3), they include the Bible as God's supernaturally inspired Word; God as a personal being above nature, sovereign, omnipotent, and unchanging; the Trinity as three eternal, distinct persons united by one essence or substance; Jesus Christ as God the Son, equal with the Father, different in kind and not only in degree from other humans, God incarnate yet truly human, the one and only savior of humankind; miracles, including the bodily resurrection of Jesus Christ; and salvation as God's loving and merciful rescue of sinful persons from hell and into an eternal relationship of blissful communion with himself in heaven. (All liberal theologians deny hell except as lack of God-consciousness and believe in universal salvation—however *salvation* is defined.) Later I will provide examples from leading liberal theologians' writings to confirm their common denials of these orthodox Christian beliefs as incompatible with reason and modern experience.

Concepts and terms such as *resurrection* are often used by liberal theologians and their Christian followers, but careful interpretation reveals that they do not mean historical and realistic events. These terms become mere symbols. This view is called symbolic realism. Jesus' resurrection is seen as

---

7. Ibid., 16.

a symbol that represents the continuing transformational power of his life and message. In symbolic realism, a symbol has the power to transform with or without any connection to a real event, past, present, or future. Modern knowledge allegedly makes belief in miracles impossible for those "in the know" about nature and science, but one in the know can still talk about a miracle in a symbolic sense, as an image with the power to transform. Virtually all liberal theologians and their Christian followers affirm the resurrection of Jesus but deny the empty tomb. For them the resurrection is a real symbol—a powerful image that is more than a mere sign.[8]

Certainly some symbols have power to transform. That is not the problem with symbolic realism. The problem is the disconnect between major Christian symbols and history. Often the symbol becomes only an image and not at all related to any historical event, except perhaps a spiritual-psychological one. Jesus Christ's bodily resurrection, as reported in the New Testament, is denied by virtually all liberal theologians, who see it as impossible from a modern, rational, scientific point of view. (Why this should be the case is curious. Nothing about modern science rules out miracles insofar as one believes in God as the author and sustainer of nature. The laws of nature were interpreted by the founders of modern science such as Johannes Kepler and Isaac Newton as regularities of God's general providence.) Orthodox Christianity, however, does not deny the power of symbols; it does deny that some Christian

---

8. Liberal theologian Paul Tillich (1886–1965) specialized in emphasizing the difference between a symbol and a sign. A symbol has power to transform; a sign does not. See Paul Tillich, *Systematic Theology: Three Volumes in One* (Chicago: Univ. of Chicago Press, 1967), 239.

symbols can be powerful without being rooted in historical events outside of individuals' or groups' inner spiritual experiences or psychological states.

Schleiermacher launched liberal Christianity and liberal theology. Who followed him? Who are the other prototypes of the tradition? After Schleiermacher came Albrecht Ritschl, another major German Protestant theologian (1822–89), whose influence led to a whole school of liberal theologians and pastors labeled Ritschlians. Ritschl wrote numerous books of theology and church history, including, most notably, *The Christian Doctrine of Justification and Reconciliation* (1870). Ritschl used the philosophy of German thinker Immanuel Kant (1724–1804) to distinguish between "facts" and "values," and Ritschl relegated religion to the realm of values. Christianity is not about facts but about values—what ought to be the case—especially the values of the kingdom of God as espoused by Jesus. Ultimately, Ritschl was unsuccessful in drawing an absolute line between facts and values, but he set in motion the liberal theological trend of reducing Christianity (and religion in general) to ethics. Christianity, he taught, was primarily about the kingdom of God on earth, a society organized by love.

Traditional orthodox doctrines and dogmas took a back seat in Ritschl's theology. When historical doctrines appeared at all, they were reconstructed to fit with modern sensibilities. He believed the Bible is not the inspired Word of God written but the record of "the apostolic circle of ideas" that points to ethical living in and for God's kingdom on earth, in society. One outstanding example of his liberalism in theology is his definition of Jesus Christ, in which he taught that when

Christians say that Jesus is God, they mean that Jesus has the *value of God* for them because he inaugurated and embodied the values of God's kingdom among people.

Ritschl was an abstruse, complicated thinker whose writings gave rise to many popular interpretations. One of his most astute and influential interpreters was German liberal theologian and church historian Adolf Harnack (1851–1930). Harnack taught theology in Germany for many years and was a public intellectual who wrote Kaiser Wilhelm's speech announcing war in 1914. A public building in Berlin is named after him. The Kaiser granted him the right to include "von" in his name so that he became Adolf von Harnack, indicating a degree of nobility. His lectures given at the University of Berlin (1899–1900) were published under the English title *What Is Christianity?* (the German title being different). It remains a classic of liberal theology. According to Harnack, the entirety of Christianity can be summed up in three simple ideas: "Firstly, the kingdom of God and its coming. Secondly, God the Father and the infinite value of the human soul. Thirdly, the higher righteousness and the commandment of love."[9] Clear from the context is that Harnack did not believe the kingdom of God is heavenly, supernatural, or future but natural and within human history. The kingdom is, he explained, "the rule of the holy God in the hearts of individuals; *it is God Himself in His power.* From this point of view everything that is dramatic in the external and historical sense has vanished; and gone, too, are all the external hopes for the future."[10]

---

9. Adolf von Harnack, *What Is Christianity?* trans. Thomas Bailey Saunders, 2nd ed. (New York: Putnam, 1901), 55.

10. Ibid., 60–61, italics in the original.

Together Ritschl and Harnack introduced into the stream of liberal theology the tendency to reduce religion to ethics, especially social ethics—the kingdom of God as the ideal social order organized by love. These were the German founders of what came to be known in America as the social gospel, whose main representative thinkers, preachers, and popularizers were Washington Gladden (1836–1918), Walter Rauschenbusch (1861–1918), and Harry Emerson Fosdick (1878–1969). Gladden wrote *Present Day Theology* (1913), among other classics of American liberal Christianity, in which he continued the influence of Ritschl and Harnack by centering modern Christianity on the idea of the kingdom of God as social transformation. Rauschenbusch wrote three main books that became extremely popular and influential among liberal Christians, even though he was quite evangelical, at least in his personal religious experience and commitments. His main book was *A Theology for the Social Gospel* (1917), in which he reinterpreted every orthodox doctrine in light of social progressivism. Fosdick pastored two churches, including Riverside Church in New York City, and taught theology at Union Theological Seminary. He was by far the most influential popularizer of liberal theology in America during the first half of the twentieth century. Although he wrote many books, he is perhaps best known for his published sermon "Shall the Fundamentalists Win? Or The New Knowledge and the Christian Faith" (1922). Fosdick thundered against fundamentalism without insisting on liberal theology, but he clearly believed classical, orthodox doctrines to be optional for Christians. He expressed the basic, unifying idea of liberal Christianity by proclaiming that "we must . . . be able to think our Christian faith clear enough in modern terms."[11]

Another early twentieth-century American liberal theologian of the Ritschlian school was Henry Churchill King (1858–1934), president of Oberlin College from 1902 to 1927. King wrote, among other books of liberal theology, *Reconstruction in Theology* (1901), in which he declared that "the acceptance of certain great convictions of our own day calls for a rewriting of theology—a new theology."[12] Most indicative of his liberal theological leanings is his description of Jesus Christ as "the Ideal realized"[13] and "the supreme self-revelation of God."[14] While these are true descriptions of Jesus Christ according to orthodox Christianity, they are insufficient ones. Nowhere does King confess the deity of Jesus Christ in orthodox terms as God incarnate.

Perhaps by now some readers are asking, "I've never heard of these people, so how can they be important to me?" The answer is that we are all influenced by people we've never heard of. These liberal theologians of the past, and the rest yet to be mentioned, presented ideas that trickle down into sermons and popular religious books and general folk religion (including folk Christianity). Sometimes these trickled-down ideas are partial, not part of a package of liberal theology. And yet even one liberal idea, such as that Jesus Christ was not divine in the same way as God, can serve as

11. Harry Emerson Fosdick, *Shall the Fundamentalists Win? Or The New Knowledge and the Christian Faith* (1922; New York: Crossreach, 2016), 6.

12. Henry Churchill King, *Reconstruction in Theology* (New York: Macmillan, 1901), 29.

13. Ibid., 245.

14. Ibid., 243.

a leaven that leavens the whole loaf of a Christian denomination or congregation or ministry or even mind. Years ago I visited a mainline Protestant megachurch and heard a sermon that I recognized as taken from the theology of liberal theologian Paul Tillich. I doubt that any of the congregants had ever heard of Tillich, and the preacher never mentioned him, but the whole sermon was straight out of Tillich's liberal theology. Countless times have I recognized liberal theology communicated implicitly through a sermon, a popular religious book, or even a cliché. Even orthodox Christians are unwittingly influenced by liberal theology.

World War I chastened the optimism of nineteenth-century European liberal theology, which had expected the kingdom of God to dawn through the social gospel and progressive social transformation. American liberal theology had to wait until World War II to experience the same chastening. After the two world wars, liberal Christians no longer hoped for or expected the kingdom of God to come on earth through the church's social efforts. Their optimism was shaken, but the other tenets of liberal Christianity remained steady.

The leading liberal theologian of the twentieth century was Paul Tillich. His influence could be compared with that of Schleiermacher, although Tillich stood on Schleiermacher's shoulders. One major difference is that Schleiermacher borrowed heavily from Romanticism in his reconstruction of Christianity, whereas Tillich called existentialism the "good luck" of Christianity in the postwar eras in Europe and America. Tillich began his theological career in Germany but escaped the Nazis to America, where he taught at Union Theological Seminary, Harvard University, and the University of Chicago Divinity School. Tillich wrote numerous books, but his magnum opus was *Systematic Theology*.[15] There he described the task of theology as "correspondence" with culture and philosophy, giving philosophy a controlling role in interpreting the symbols of Christianity. He denied that Jesus Christ had to have existed as the person described in the Gospels. He insisted that someone who embodied the "new being"—but not necessarily Jesus—had to be behind the gospel stories. He denied that Jesus Christ, whoever he was, rose bodily from the dead. Instead, Tillich interpreted the resurrection as the "restitution" of the disciples' faith in the message of Jesus Christ, a message that everyone is capable of overcoming despair by realizing that they are accepted by God, who is Being itself.

In addition to Tillich's theology came process theology, which borrowed heavily from the philosophy of Alfred North Whitehead (1861–1947). Its main American proponent was Methodist theologian John Cobb (b. 1925), author of numerous books of liberal theology and liberal Christianity. Cobb and other process theologians reconstructed Christianity to be compatible with naturalism—the worldview that nature is all there is. In process theology, God is a deep dimension of nature, guiding it, especially humans, toward greater realizations of beauty and harmony. Lutheran theologian Robert Jenson quipped that the only thing wrong with process theology is that it is such an attractive alternative to Christian faith—because process theology denies the omnipotence of God, reducing God to the great cosmic persuader toward

---

15. Paul Tillich, *Systematic Theology*, 3 vols. (Chicago: Univ. of Chicago Press, 1951–63).

beauty and harmony. According to process theology, God is the "fellow sufferer who understands" (Whitehead), but God can change things only through persuasion. Ultimately, everything that exists, including God's own inner experience, depends on creatures' free realizations of God's "initial aims." The appeal of process theology is that it solves the old problem of evil by robbing God of coercive power; God can only persuade, not cause or prevent. Process theologians do not believe in miracles, including the bodily resurrection of Jesus Christ, or the inspiration and authority of the Bible, although they express respect for the Bible as stories sacred to Christians.

Other influential American liberal theologians include Methodist L. Harold DeWolf (1905–86), Peter C. Hodgson (b. 1934), Donald E. Miller (b. 1946), John Shelby Spong (1931–2021), and Marcus Borg (1942–2015). All five have written influential books, and Spong and Borg appear in several YouTube videos debating conservative Christians about the historicity of Christ's resurrection and talking about liberal theology versus conservative theology. Spong and Borg are almost certainly the most influential popularizers of liberal theology among Christians in the past four to five decades. Spong, as a retired Episcopal bishop, made a late career out of appearing on television and radio talk shows to blast conservative religion and promote his own brand of liberal Christianity.

Two major interpreters of American liberal Christianity besides Dorrien are the aforementioned Kenneth Cauthen (b. 1930) and William R. Hutchison (1930–2005). Both wrote major studies of American liberal theology. Cauthen wrote *The Impact of American Religious Liberalism* (1962), and Hutchison wrote *The Modernist Impulse in American Protestantism* (1976).

Cauthen wrote of liberalism in religion and theology that it is "a distinct theological perspective, within which there are divergences of emphasis with regard to both method and content."[16] Yet he also wrote about certain unifying perspectives among theological-religious liberals, especially their emphasis on God's immanence and denial of "special, miraculous revelations."[17] Cauthen also noted liberal religion's view of Jesus Christ as "the perfection of human personality," such that his "divinity is his perfect humanity."[18] According to Cauthen, these and other common themes unify liberal Christian beliefs in spite of different perspectives on some minor issues.

Hutchison identified three "enduring modernist ideas" in liberal Christianity: cultural involvement, adaptationism, and divine immanence.[19] The first two refer to liberal theology's insistence on accommodating Christianity to modernism. The third refers to liberal theology's distinctive emphasis on God's presence in the world process as opposed to God's transcendence over it. Classical, orthodox Christianity has always emphasized both God's immanence and God's transcendence, God's presence within and involvement with the world, including nature, *and* God's holy otherness, freedom, sovereignty, and power. Liberal theology emphasizes the former to the neglect of the latter.[20]

Cauthen and Hutchison, along with Dorrien, remain three of the most astute and influential expositors of modern

---

16. Kenneth Cauthen, *The Impact of American Religious Liberalism*, 2nd ed. (1962; Lanham, MD: Univ. Press of America, 1983), 209.

17. Ibid., 209, 210.

18. Ibid., 211.

19. William R. Hutchison, *The Modernist Impulse in American Protestantism* (New York and Oxford: Oxford Univ. Press, 1976), 311.

20. See chapter 4 below for more on the doctrine of God.

liberal Christianity, and their careful, relatively objective, well-researched thoughts about that religious tradition remain influential in understanding the unity and diversity of the tradition. Although none of them argues that liberal Christianity is not authentic Christianity, orthodox Christians reading their books cannot help but conclude that the liberal Christianity they describe is an entirely different religion from orthodox Christianity—as Machen argued in 1923 in *Christianity and Liberalism*.[21]

The upshot of all this is simple: liberal Christianity is a relatively unified, new religion growing out of orthodox Christianity and, like sects such as Mormonism, Christian Science, and Jehovah's Witnesses, growing away from it. Like these Christian offshoots, liberal Christianity cut the cord of continuity with New Testament Christianity, ancient Christianity (of the church fathers), Reformation Christianity, and even Catholic and Eastern Orthodox Christianity. Liberalism is to contemporary Christianity what Gnosticism was to second century Christianity—an alternative religion to true Christianity.

---

21. Hutchison especially discusses Machen's book and the surprising agreement with its argument by public intellectual and secular humanist Walter Lippmann. According to Hutchison, "What made liberalism 'another religion,'" for Machen, "was, above all, its disbelief in the supernatural Christ-events" (Hutchison, *Modernist Impulse in American Protestantism*, 265).

CHAPTER 2

LIBERAL THEOLOGY'S
SOURCES AND NORMS

Looking at liberal Christianity and orthodox Christianity side by side is like comparing apples and oranges. Or humans and orangutans. There are certain similarities, but they are different species. Both apples and oranges are fruits; humans and orangutans are primates. But for all their similarities, they are not the same. A better example would probably be the World Council of Churches, which is an extremely diverse organization but still affirms that Jesus Christ is God and savior, and the Church of Jesus Christ of Latter-Day Saints, for whom Jesus Christ is God and savior but not eternal God. On the surface they seem to belong to the same species, but beneath the similar language they mean different things.[1] And

---

1. I have read a great deal of Latter-Day Saints literature and have engaged in dialogue with Latter-Day Saints religion scholars at Brigham Young University several times. I have also invited Latter-Day Saints directors of Institutes of Religion into my classes over the years. When I have asked them directly whether they believe Jesus Christ has always been God, eternally equal with the Father, they have uniformly

the deepest difference between orthodox Christianity and liberal Christianity has to do with their differing sources and norms for belief.

I have never read or heard the basic difference between orthodox Christianity and liberal Christianity expressed more clearly and concisely than by liberal theologian Delwin Brown, whom I quoted in the introduction. According to Brown, the main difference between orthodox Christianity and liberal Christianity has to do with different authorities for belief. Liberal Christianity's main authority for belief is "the modern consensus," by which Brown means contemporary "reason, sensory experience, intuition, . . . praxis," and not the Bible. He wrote, "To summarize my view, the Bible is not the criterion of truth. . . . The Bible does not 'norm' us, it does form us."[2] Clark Pinnock, an orthodox Christian theologian, responded that the main problem with liberal theology is "its apparent willingness to break with the foundational proclamation. . . . It leaves the way open to reduce and distort the Word of God under the pressure of modern ideas."[3] Brown responded to Pinnock's orthodox defense of the Bible as Christianity's supreme source and norm for belief by saying, "I do not think anyone should ever believe anything simply because it is in the Bible."[4]

---

said no. I asked an official of the National Council of Churches whether the Church of Jesus Christ of Latter-Day Saints is or could be a member denomination and she said no. Admittedly, some people will disagree with me about this, but that Latter-Day Saints are not Christians (which is not a judgment about their salvation!) is my considered opinion based on much reflection and study.

2. Clark H. Pinnock and Delwin Brown, *Theological Crossfire: An Evangelical/Liberal Dialogue* (Grand Rapids: Zondervan, 1990), 28, 29.

3. Ibid., 36.

4. Ibid., 109.

Brown's stance on the Bible's authority echoes Schleiermacher's and that of every liberal theologian I have mentioned so far. Each would put it differently, but all agree that the Bible "norms us" rather than being our primary source and norm for belief. What does that mean? Hopefully that will become clearer as we go on through this exposition and critique of liberal Christianity. For now, however, I will say that to me it means that the Bible gives us certain symbols and images that shape our Christian character but is not the supreme authority for beliefs about God, humanity, salvation, the future, and other crucial religious ideas. Overriding the Bible and orthodox Christian tradition is the perceived modern, contemporary experience, especially of scholars, many of them secular humanists.

This is an appropriate place to stop to discuss the issue of facts arising from scientific research versus what we read in the Bible about nature. Virtually all modern orthodox Christians agree that if something is true, a settled fact, it cannot be denied. "Don't confuse me with the facts; my mind is already made up" may be a declaration appealing to anti-intellectual Christians (and I have heard it declared at the close of more than one sermon!), but it is not a viable attitude toward true facts (as opposed to mere theories or opinions). If something is a brute, material fact, whatever its source may be, it belongs to God. "All truth is God's truth" is a fundamental belief of orthodox Christianity going back to the church fathers.[5] A conservative, evangelical theologian such as Bernard Ramm (1916–92) has persuasively argued in books like *The Christian View of Science and Scripture* (1954) that orthodox Christianity

---

5. See orthodox Christian philosopher Arthur F. Holmes's book *All Truth Is God's Truth* (Grand Rapids: Eerdmans, 1977).

does not ignore science or regard science as an enemy. The issue is not the Bible or orthodox Christianity versus scientific facts; if the Bible seems to conflict with a fact, then orthodox Christians have always been willing to reinterpret the Bible. Our interpretations may be wrong, but that does not falsify or undermine the authority of the Bible for doctrines and beliefs about God and Jesus Christ. Nothing science could ever discover as fact could conflict with basic Christian beliefs such as the existence of the triune God, the incarnation of God in Jesus Christ, the resurrection of Jesus Christ, or salvation by grace alone through faith.

The key doctrinal beliefs of orthodox Christianity, as spelled out and defended in books like C. S. Lewis's *Mere Christianity* and John Stott's *Basic Christianity*, are rooted in the Bible and cannot be undermined by science or philosophy. Conflict with Christianity arises only when scientists and philosophers are predisposed to rule out anything above or beyond nature, and this predisposition is a bias, not an objective fact or knowledge. The problem for orthodox Christianity is not science but naturalism.[6] Naturalism is the worldview that presupposes that nature is all that exists, which is a belief not proven or sustained by science, even if many scientists have adopted it.

For classical, orthodox Christianity of every variety, Eastern Orthodox, Roman Catholic, and Protestant, the Bible has always been considered the supreme source and norm for basic Christian belief about God, Jesus Christ, humanity, salvation, and the future. Yes, to be sure, Eastern Orthodoxy

---

6. See Alvin Plantinga, *Where the Conflict Really Lies: Science, Religion, and Naturalism* (New York: Oxford Univ. Press, 2011).

and Roman Catholicism add certain extrabiblical traditions to their beliefs as sources and norms for doctrines, but they argue that none of it conflicts with the Bible. When it comes down to identifying the primary source and norm for basic Christian theology, doctrines, beliefs, all orthodox Christians turn to the Bible as rightly interpreted and do not believe that cultural consensus trumps the Bible on God, Jesus Christ, humanity, salvation, and the future.

Liberal Christianity elevates modern reason and experience to sources and norms that trump the Bible and orthodox Christian tradition. So much so that Scripture and tradition are demoted to being helpful spiritual guides. For liberal Christians, the Bible is a reservoir of influential symbols and images and a record of the original Christians' experiences. It consists of "our sacred stories," but it is not supernaturally inspired or infallible—even in matters of doctrine, Christian teaching, beliefs about God, etcetera. The result is a severely negotiated, altered, adapted, accommodated belief system that is called Christian but is cut off from anything recognized as Christian by any Christian thinker or leader before Schleiermacher.

Liberal theologian Dorrien asks whether "Christian theology can be genuinely Christian without being based upon external authority."[7] His implicit answer is yes, and he regards this as the core of true liberal theology: "The essential idea of liberal theology is that all claims to truth, in theology as in other disciplines, must be made on the basis of reason and

---

7. Gary J. Dorrien, *The Making of American Liberal Theology: Imagining Progressive Religion, 1805–1900* (Louisville: Westminster John Knox, 2001), xiii.

experience, not by appeal to external authority."[8] By "external authority" he means Scripture and tradition, not only church authorities such as the pope or a bishop or a denominational leader. Dorrien sums up the bedrock identity of liberal theology, including liberal Christianity in its intellectual form, this way: "One way or another, liberal theology always took its stand on the verdicts of modern knowledge and experience without bowing to external authority claims. . . . They specialized in cultural accommodation and religious progressivism. Every liberal theologian sought to bring Christian claims into line with beliefs derived from modern critical consciousness."[9] Here Dorrien sums up liberal Christian theology in the past tense, as if that were not true of today's version of the tradition, but elsewhere he makes clear that this basic approach is and has always been true of liberal theology.

If reason and experience, meaning the best of contemporary philosophy and science and religious experience, are authoritative for liberal Christianity, the question remains, Whose reason and experience and which religious experiences are the sources and norms for contemporary life and belief? With this approach to religious authority, how does one avoid radical individualism, even anarchy? Is Christianity endlessly flexible, changeable, mutable? Is everyone's "hat" his or her own church? How much can an individual Christian's beliefs differ, be unique to him or her, while maintaining that we have one God, one faith, and one universal church? On what ground can a Christian leader say about a self-proclaimed prophet

---

8. Gary J. Dorrien, *The Making of American Liberal Theology: Idealism, Realism, and Modernity, 1900–1950* (Louisville: Westminster John Knox, 2003), 1.

9. Ibid., 534.

from Korea, for example, "No, he is not the 'Lord of the Second Advent'"? How does the Christian leader know that the Korean prophet is a false prophet if many of his followers experience him as a true prophet and if his truth claims and doctrines are not easily falsifiable by modern thought? This might seem like a far-fetched example, but in the 1970s some liberal Protestant theologians expressed sympathy with that Korean prophet and his followers.

However, one does not need to go to such an extreme case to make my point that liberal Christianity is not authentic Christianity. The following chapters about liberal views about God and Jesus Christ will make that case. Liberal Christian theology is a different species from biblical, historical, classical, orthodox Christianity *because* it has cut itself off from all authority except that of the individual's self and modern thought, and modern thought is basically secular.

The plain fact is that, in this writer's considered opinion, liberal Christian theologians and their followers have drifted away from authentic Christianity either without knowing it or without wanting to acknowledge it. They don't want to stop calling themselves Christians, so they baptize what they now believe as Christianity while redefining Christianity so radically that it can't reasonably be recognized as continuous with biblical, historical, classical, orthodox Christianity. It is a new, invented religion with roots in Christianity—exactly like many sects and cults of Christianity whose members call themselves Christians but are not recognized as such even by the World Council of Churches.

Kenneth Cauthen agrees with Dorrien that for liberal Christian theology, "No special, miraculous revelations are necessary"[10] to be truly Christian. According to Cauthen, liberals' knowledge of God comes through experience.[11] What experience? "The victory of spirit over nature" that happens when people "appropriate the light and life which are mediated to them through the impact of the historical Jesus."[12] In other words, "Christian belief" is what reasonably follows when a person thinks about his or her inward transformation brought about by encounter with the historical Jesus through his teachings and through his living influence in the church. This is exactly what Schleiermacher taught two centuries before: true salvation is the inward increase of God-consciousness through the influence of Jesus through the Bible and the church. But from Schleiermacher on, liberal theology has voided this experience of any unifying cognitive content that defines Christianity. Doctrines are reduced to opinions, at most expressions of inner experiences. They carry no authority and are always revisable in light of contemporary culture. The result is that when you visit a liberal congregation, you cannot know what the members believe, only what they don't believe. For example, they typically don't believe that faith in the supernatural, such as Jesus' resurrection or other miracles, is necessary for authentic Christianity.[13]

Several liberal theologians confirm that experience, reason, and culture are liberal Christianity's authoritative

---

10. Kenneth Cauthen, *The Impact of American Religious Liberalism*, 2nd ed. (1962; Lanham, MD: Univ. Press of America, 1983), 210.

11. Ibid.

12. Ibid., 211.

13. Lutheran sociologist of religion Peter Berger is quoted in Gary J. Dorrien, *The Making of American Liberal Theology: Crisis, Irony, and Postmodernity, 1950–2005* (Louisville: Westminster John Knox, 2006), as saying that in liberal theology "every form of supernaturalism must be expunged from Christianity" (518).

sources. Washington Gladden wrote in 1913 that "the present day theology . . . is simply the explanation which men are giving of religious truth in the light of this century."[14] By "this century" he almost certainly meant the twentieth century as he envisioned it unfolding in progress with science and modern culture. "Our modern way of looking at things" was for him at least equal to Scripture and tradition for establishing right belief.[15] Gladden was a cautious liberal pastor and theologian who was not in the vanguard of extreme liberal theology, but he called for a "courageous radicalism" in interpretation of the Bible in light of modern knowledge.[16] Such must be combined, he said, with a "wise conservation" of tradition.[17] Most liberal Christian theologians would say the same; they rarely admit to throwing out tradition entirely and probably never do that. Their selections of what to believe and teach from tradition are always influenced strongly by their reception of modern or contemporary culture, meaning the best of philosophy and the sciences.

Henry Churchill King was, like Gladden, less than radical in his reinterpretations of Christianity, but even King affirmed that "all doctrine should be originally only the thought expression of experience."[18] These "thought expressions" ought to be shaped by the "changed intellectual, moral, and spiritual world in which we live."[19] "Theology must grow as science

14. Washington Gladden, *Present Day Theology* (Columbus, OH: McClelland, 1913), 8.

15. Ibid., 44.

16. Ibid., 20.

17. Ibid.

18. Henry Churchill King, *Reconstruction in Theology* (New York: Macmillan, 1901), 182.

19. Ibid., v.

grows."[20] While warning against the weakening of "the hold
of all Christian truth" through a strong "protest against the
old creeds," King argued that "the acceptance of certain great
convictions of our own day calls for a rewriting of theology—a
new theology."[21] How he worked this out will be explained in
later chapters. The point here is that he called for a new theology shaped in part, at least, by modern thought. The result
was profound change especially in the doctrines of God and
Jesus Christ.

Methodist theologian L. Harold DeWolf was another relatively cautious liberal theologian who at least paid lip service to
tradition, not wishing to throw the proverbial baby out with the
bathwater. Nevertheless, in his classic *The Case for Theology in
Liberal Perspective*, he urged that "the mood and thought of our
age . . . require that the gospel be communicated in terms intel-
ligible and persuasive to twentieth-century minds."[22] Against
what he regarded as a new rise of irrationality in Protestant theology, DeWolf emphasized reason without precisely explaining
what that means except in terms of "the natural sciences" and
"the new historical understanding of Biblical times."[23] Against
theologies that he regarded as anti-intellectual and antiquated,
he called for a cautious accommodation of Christianity to modern culture.[24] DeWolf was typical of most liberal theologians of
his day in attempting to distinguish between the kernel and
the husk of Christianity, with the husk being disposable and

20. Ibid., 2.
21. Ibid., 29.
22. L. Harold DeWolf, *The Case for Theology in Liberal Perspective* (Philadelphia:
Westminster, 1959), 43.
23. Ibid., 45.
24. Ibid., 58.

the kernel being kept. For him, as for most liberal theologians, the kernel is the "ethical requirements of Jesus," while the husk is the "moral customs of the day"—meaning of Jesus' time.[25] However, a reader of his book cannot be blamed for thinking that his husk also includes much of traditional, orthodox doctrine. This will be made clear with examples in later chapters.

Donald E. Miller, author of *The Case for Liberal Christianity*, expresses the liberal theological emphasis on modern culture very clearly:

> Liberal Christians have understood that Christianity must evolve and adapt itself—or at least its expression—from age to age. They have believed that the application of the gospel must be reinterpreted from each new cultural context. Although there may be a core essence of Christianity, liberal Christians view accommodation to culture as necessary and positive, if what one means by "accommodation" is that they should seek to understand God and their moral responsibility in terms of the best available scientific knowledge and social analysis.[26]

Miller says, "Although Scripture and tradition are important, the basepoint of liberal morality has been reason. . . . Always reason is to be used in weighing the authority of Scripture and tradition."[27] No conservative Christian rejects reason entirely; the issue is whose reason? Which rational-

---

25. Ibid., 146.
26. Donald E. Miller, *The Case for Liberal Christianity* (San Francisco: Harper and Row, 1981), 33.
27. Ibid., 35.

ity? Conservative Christians have always valued logic; that is not the issue. Miller means more than logic by "reason" as the criterion of authority; he almost certainly means the best of modern thought, especially the modern and contemporary sciences and the arts.[28] Once again, conservative, orthodox Christians do not necessarily reject the sciences and arts or even philosophy; we reject elevating those to equality with Scripture and tradition in determining what is right for Christians to believe about God and Jesus Christ.

Miller displays his liberal leaning toward cultural accommodation in discussing the status of beliefs in Christianity. He embraces what was earlier called symbolic realism and says that he can recite the creeds of Christianity without taking them literally.[29] He confesses being agnostic about miracles: "I have given up on trying to settle the question of the resurrection, whether Jesus was born of a virgin, whether he made the blind see and the lame walk."[30] According to him and many, if not most, if not all, liberal theologians, the Scriptures and creeds are symbolic landmarks or milestones not to be interpreted literally; they are fictional in form while true in substance.[31] But how does he identify the difference between form and substance? Apparently by what modern-contemporary culture allows in terms of literal-historical truth and reality. So what is the substance for him? It is "the Reality" which lies behind the forms and which is mediated by them and one's experience of it.[32] So why the church? According to Miller the church is "united by

---

28. Ibid., 33.
29. Ibid., 5.
30. Ibid.
31. Ibid., 15.
32. Ibid., 31.

a common symbolic paradigm,"[33] which has something to do with "a Reality" we experience "both within and beyond our humanly created symbols."[34]

Can anyone really be blamed for wondering what religion this is? Is Miller's liberal Christianity *Christian*? What makes his theology and religion Christian? According to him, it is "the symbolic form of Jesus," which is not bound by time but is subject to reinterpretation by the liberal church in every age and generation.[35] The symbolic form of Jesus is apparently the key to "human wholeness . . . confidence in the ultimate meaningfulness of human existence."[36] More of Miller's thoughts about liberal Christianity will appear in later chapters. Here it should suffice to say that, in true liberal theological fashion, he accommodates Christianity to his vision of what contemporary culture will allow one to believe. All orthodox Christians will question whether the result is recognizable as Christianity.

Liberal Christian theologian John Shelby Spong asked whether it is still possible "to be a believer and a citizen of our [twentieth] century at the same time."[37] For him, "When the modern age began to dawn, a new understanding of the shape of the universe began to grow and God's place as the heavenly director of human affairs began to totter."[38] He concluded, "Divine intervention became a problematic concept."[39] Finally,

33. Ibid., 10.
34. Ibid., 20.
35. Ibid., 137.
36. Ibid., 37.
37. John Shelby Spong, *Why Christianity Must Change or Die: A Bishop Speaks to Believers in Exile* (San Francisco: HarperSanFrancisco, 1998), 18.
38. Ibid., 31.
39. Ibid., 32.

he declared, "Human beings have evolved to the place where the theistic God concept can be and must be cast aside."[40] There can be little doubt that for Spong, a retired Episcopal bishop, theologian, and author of numerous books of liberal Christianity, the modern worldview—naturalistic in essence, closed to miracles—stands as a major source and norm even over "treasured biblical tales" that constitute "history . . . interpreted in rather dramatic and fanciful ways."[41] For him, as for many, if not most, liberal Christians, the best of modern thought serves as a ruling norm for Christian belief. The Bible is still a source, but contemporary philosophy and science decide what parts of it are true and what parts are not. For him, Christianity must change or die, and the change he advocates is one that takes Christianity far from traditional orthodoxy. In this writer's opinion, he cuts the cord of continuity so thoroughly that what is left of his "changed Christianity" is unrecognizable as Christian.

Liberal theologian Marcus Borg expressed a desire to revision Christianity by rethinking God under the influence of the modern worldview, taking seriously contemporary culture while at the same time remaining consistent with the theological tradition of Christianity.[42] Whether the outcome of his revisioning actually is consistent with Christianity's theological tradition is questionable. One example is his objection to "creedal Jesus,"[43] by which he means the traditional Christology of ecumenical, historical, orthodox Christianity:

---

40. Ibid., 54.
41. Ibid., 14, 15.
42. Marcus J. Borg, *The God We Never Knew: Beyond Dogmatic Religion to a More Authentic Contemporary Faith* (New York: HarperCollins, 1997), 4, 1.
43. Ibid., 97.

Jesus Christ is both truly God and truly human, yet one person. For him, modern thought has made it difficult, if not impossible, to believe that "the pre-Easter Jesus was divine."[44] Sentences such as "in our time, thinking about God as a supernatural being 'out there' has become an obstacle for many"[45] reveal his commitment to what people of the modern age can believe. His book titled *The God We Never Knew: Beyond Dogmatic Religion to a More Authentic Contemporary Faith* (1997) is based on the authority of modernity (although he does not like the word *authority*), even in revisioning Christianity.

Peter C. Hodgson, author of *Liberal Theology: A Radical Vision* (2007), stands out as an exception to Dorrien's claim that liberal Christianity has no need of external authority. He writes, "Theology cannot dispense with external authority and historical tradition,"[46] but then also writes that "our time" calls for a radical revisioning of traditional Christianity open to "experience: empirical, sensible, emotional, intuitive, intellectual, aesthetic, cultural, revelatory."[47] His true theologically liberal colors show when he writes that "a radically free liberal theology is [called] to free central doctrines of the Christian faith from dogmatic or antiquated forms and rethink their root meanings in relation to contemporary conceptualities and issues."[48]

Douglas Ottati has emerged as one of the most articulate and prolific liberal theologians of the twenty-first century. In his magnum opus, *A Theology for the Twenty-First Century*,

---

44. Ibid., 91.
45. Ibid., 12.
46. Peter Crafts Hodgson, *Liberal Theology: A Radical Vision* (Minneapolis: Fortress, 2007), 9.
47. Ibid., 19, 14.
48. Ibid., 29.

he endorses the Wesleyan Quadrilateral for Christian theology's sources and norms. The volume is divided into seventy propositions, and proposition twenty-four indicates that "theological statements or doctrines will be formulated with reference to the Scripture of the Old and New Testaments, church history or tradition (confessions, practices, and past theological formulations), contemporary knowledge, and consistency with other theological statements."[49] After cautioning readers not to rely solely or too much on "current knowledge and beliefs," Ottati says, "Even so, appeals to contemporary knowledge, theories, and beliefs are especially important if Christian doctrines are to offer reinterpretations—with respect to God—of our current life and interactions with objects and others."[50] Throughout his theological reflections for the twenty-first century, Ottati heavily relies on what he calls "theocentric piety," which turns out to be very similar to Schleiermacher's "God-consciousness." Theocentric piety is the Christian experience of God that gives life meaning, depth, and hope, and it is "encouraged" by "the mythopoeic resources of the Bible and Christian tradition,"[51] which contain symbols rather than literal events or propositional teachings (although nowhere does Ottati deny that such exist). The upshot is that for Ottati, as for many if not most liberal Christian thinkers, the ultimate sources for knowledge about God, Jesus Christ, humanity, salvation, and the various loci of Christian theology are not supernaturally delivered revelations in salvation

---

49. Douglas F. Ottati, *A Theology for the Twenty-First Century* (Grand Rapids: Eerdmans, 2020), 126.

50. Ibid., 135.

51. Ibid., 323.

history as recorded in Scripture or authoritative teachings of inspired prophets and apostles; instead, that knowledge originates from biblical symbols and Christians' inner experiences inspired by them. And the best of modern knowledge serves as critical guide to what it is possible to believe about history and nature, including miracles.

At the end of this tour of liberal Christian thinkers and their sources and norms for contemporary Christian belief, I come back to Delwin Brown, who asserts that what unites all liberal Christians is their "obligation to . . . talk about God in relation to contemporary knowledge and in terms of contemporary criteria of adequacy."[52] For them, Brown insists, "the modern consensus" has supreme authority for Christian theology,[53] at least alongside if not above Scripture and tradition.

Liberal theologian Van Harvey looked back over nearly two centuries of liberal Christian thought and commented that for it, "'Christianity' became merely a re-presentation of modern self-understanding."[54] Even I would not go quite that far! It's interesting, though, that a highly regarded liberal Christian theologian would say that about contemporary liberal Christianity. What I do believe is that liberal Christians elevate temporary, passing intellectual fashions of Western culture to the status of controlling authority for what they believe. It's understandable; educated, sophisticated people don't want to be out of touch with what academic culture considers believable or unbelievable. There comes a point,

---

52. Pinnock and Brown, *Theological Crossfire*, 87.

53. Ibid., 23.

54. Quoted in Dorrien, *Making of American Liberal Theology: Crisis, Irony, and Postmodernity*, 516.

however, where a line has been crossed from the essence of Christianity into something else. Liberal Christian theologians have constantly redefined the "essence of Christianity" to defend their new religion as authentically Christian. But since Schleiermacher, that essence has been whittled down to something unrecognizable as Christian—except for the language, the words, the terminology.

Liberal Christians still speak of God and Jesus Christ, and they pay lip service to Bible, Trinity, sin, and salvation, but their new definitions empty those concepts of what Christians have always meant. To be sure, orthodox Christians have had and still have disagreements about the details of these concepts, but they have agreed on essential meanings. God, for example, traditionally has been seen as the personal and omnipotent creator of all things, self-existent, omniscient, omnipresent, and sovereign. Orthodox Christians debate the exact meanings of some of these concepts about God, but they agree, for example, that God is not dependent on the world for his being or existence and that God is transcendent. Liberal theology, as I will demonstrate, has overemphasized God's immanence (being in and with the world) to the point of losing God's transcendence. And that is true because liberal Christians think modern, contemporary culture no longer allows God to be transcendent.

CHAPTER 3

LIBERAL THEOLOGY
AND THE BIBLE

Orthodox Christians of many denominations and traditions have disagreed for centuries about the details of the
Bible. We disagree about how many books should be in it, but
we all agree on sixty-six of them. Some think there should be
and really are more (books of the so-called Apocrypha between
the two testaments). Some think the Old Testament and the
New Testament stand in greater unity theologically than others
do. Some view the Old Testament as history and promise leading up to the coming of God's self-revelation in Jesus Christ.
Some believe in the plenary verbal inspiration of the Bible while
others believe *inspiration* refers to the Holy Spirit's work with
the human authors, the words themselves not being inspired.
Some believe the Bible is inerrant; others prefer to say it is infallible. But whether an orthodox Christian is Eastern Orthodox or
Roman Catholic or Protestant, he or she believes the Bible is different in kind and not just in degree from other books. All agree

that it is a sacred and holy book, inspired by God as is no other book, and authoritative for faith and practice (ethics).

None of that is intended to minimize the differences among orthodox Christians about the Bible. The differences are profound and unfortunate. But the consensus is even greater than the differences. The consensus—from the apostles (about the Old Testament) to the church fathers up to contemporary times—is that the Bible is supernatural in its revelatory status and authoritative for Christian thinking and living. To be sure, non-Protestants elevate tradition alongside the Bible, but that does not mean they don't believe the Bible to be uniquely inspired and authoritative compared with other great books of spiritual wisdom. They do.

This chapter begins a series on particular beliefs, doctrines, of Christianity. This book's thesis is that liberal Christianity has cut the cord of continuity with the Christian past, orthodoxy, so thoroughly that it ought to be considered a different religion. Beginning with this chapter, *some degree of familiarity on the part of the reader with orthodox Christianity across denominational boundaries is assumed.* For those who do not have that, I suggest my book *The Mosaic of Christian Belief,* which provides details about the Christian consensus, as well as about alternatives to it and diverse opinions within it.[1] In each chapter, I will mention and briefly describe the orthodox consensual doctrine before and as I describe and critique liberal Christianity's alternative view. But I will not provide details about that orthodox consensus; I will assume some basic knowledge of it.

1. Roger E. Olson, *The Mosaic of Christian Belief: Twenty Centuries of Unity and Diversity,* 2nd ed. (Downers Grove, IL: InterVarsity Press, 2016).

Most simply stated, the orthodox Christian doctrine of the Bible is that it is supernaturally inspired by God and even infallible and authoritative in all matters pertaining to salvation—broadly defined as persons' relationship with God and personal fulfillment. It is unique among books because it is God's Word written, different in kind, not just in degree, from other great books. This belief in the special status of the Bible is found in the Bible itself (e.g., 2 Tim. 3:16–17; 2 Peter 1:20–21) and throughout church history from the church fathers up to the modern era of Western thought, when deists, for example, began to question the Bible's inspiration and authority.

Compared with the orthodox Christian consensus that the Bible is the supernaturally given revelation of God, liberal Christianity treats the Bible as a human book of great insight and spiritual wisdom that is not divinely inspired or uniquely authoritative. To be sure, as I will show, many liberal theologians have said what they consider to be complimentary things about the Bible, but what they have said falls far short of acknowledging the Bible's status in traditional Christianity. The underlying reason is liberals' tendency to deny any supernatural interventions or special acts in history, including authoring the Bible through human writers. It's almost impossible to state a consensus among liberal Christian theologians about the Bible except by saying what it is *not* to them. However, I believe most would agree with the statement that the Bible constitutes the literary "Christian classic" and "our sacred stories" and that its special function lies in presenting us with the experiences of Israel and the earliest Christians and communicating to us transforming images and symbols that can and should norm our living. Liberal Christians are extremely reluctant, however, to talk about the Bible's authority, and that leaves them without an objective source or norm for Christian belief and doctrine.

Many liberal Christian theologians (and those influenced by them) have concluded from higher criticism that the Bible cannot be trusted to be what Christians believed about it for centuries. Higher criticism began in the eighteenth century in Europe but really took off among academic biblical scholars in the nineteenth century. And it evolved further during the twentieth century up to and including the Jesus Seminar of which Marcus Borg was a member. Higher criticism approaches the study of the Bible as ancient literature and refuses to engage in "special pleading" for it. The practitioners of higher criticism set aside faith in the Bible as God's Word written and seek to examine its origins, evolution, and meaning using secular techniques of literary criticism. Higher criticism has not achieved much by way of consensus about the Bible, except that it is thoroughly human in origin and radically conditioned by cultures and traditions.

Biblical scholarship is not the problem; the problem is higher criticism's naturalistic assumption, which colors and conditions how critics see the Bible. For example, most higher critics of the Old Testament assume that prophetic foretelling of the future cannot be real, so if a prophet is recorded as foretelling a future political event or war, that prophet's writing must not really be his. The book attributed to the prophet must have been written later—after the events foretold. For example, most higher critics of the New Testament assume that Jesus was not divine, not God incarnate, so his words about future events must really be about events that happened before or during the times the Gospels were written. Higher critics of the New Testament assume that much of what Jesus is quoted as saying in the Gospels was invented by later Christians and read back into the mouth of Jesus when the Gospels were being written. Often in higher criticism, the purpose of the Gospels was not to record what Jesus actually said but to have Jesus saying and doing things that solved problems in the later churches where the Gospels were written.

Yet conservative, orthodox Christians should not reject higher criticism of the Bible out of hand; it has given us some interesting insights into the reasons for differences between the Gospels. One form of higher New Testament criticism is called redaction criticism, and it demonstrates that the gospel writers had theological purposes for recording certain sayings of Jesus differently from each other. Higher criticism has revealed, for example, that the gospels of Matthew and Mark almost certainly used a source called Q (for "Quelle" or "source") that no longer exists—except in the material those two gospels share in common. The problem with higher criticism is when it undermines the truth of the Bible using naturalistic assumptions about the impossibility of miracles and of God's supernaturally inspiring prophets to foretell future events.

Liberal Christianity has been profoundly influenced by what I will call "negative higher criticism of the Bible," meaning biblical scholarship working with and from naturalistic assumptions about reality. I think it is fair to say that almost the whole problem with liberal Christianity is its bias against anything that goes beyond what the sciences could ever explain. Liberal Christianity is Christianity stripped of the

57

supernatural dimension, Christianity without miracles or divine interventions.

To be sure, most liberal Christians have always believed and taught that God works in mysterious ways within people's inner spiritual and psychological worlds. For example, Schleiermacher believed that God works to create or elevate "God-consciousness" within people, but he denied miracles as incompatible with the new knowledge about physics being discovered during the Enlightenment and scientific revolutions. A generally skeptical attitude toward miracles and special divine acts pervades liberal Christianity, even as liberal Christians talk about spiritual formation in the internal lives of Christians. A favorite saying among liberal Christians—which has even leaked into conservative, orthodox Christianity!—is that prayer does not change things but only changes me. In the Bible and much of Christian tradition, however, petitionary prayer has radically changed people's lives in outward ways and has even made a difference in the physical world. But that is typically not what liberal Christians believe about prayer because they do not think that the physical world of nature is open to the miraculous.

By approaching the Bible with a naturalistic lens, liberal Christians strip it of supernatural inspiration and reduce it to a Christian classic that is fictional but nevertheless inspiring and even transforming. The Bible becomes primarily parabolic in nature. And most liberal Christians will admit that God illuminated the minds of the human authors as they opened themselves to his work in their lives. But, again, the Bible gets treated as different in degree and not different in kind from other great books of inspiring wisdom. Liberals typically view the Bible as inspired insofar as it is inspiring. But authority does not come into their biblical scholarship.

Again, I could begin with Schleiermacher and work up through other nineteenth- and twentieth-century German liberal theologians, but I want to focus on American theology—which has spread around the world through missions and social work and publishing. This book is mainly about American liberal Christianity and its theology, its beliefs. This chapter develops from the previous chapter and will inevitably repeat some of that because the underlying issue here, as there, is authority for believing. What is or ought to be our ultimate, final authority for what we believe about God, Jesus Christ, the human condition, salvation, the future? That is the underlying and overall question, and I showed the consensus answer of liberal Christian theologians in the previous chapter. It is, in brief, modernity. Here I will focus on the authority of the Bible, or lack of it, in liberal Christianity.

Some readers may ask, "What about the fact that the Bible is interpreted in so many different ways even by conservative, traditional, orthodox Christians?" The implication is that the diversity of interpretations somehow undermines the authority of the Bible. I want to set this objection aside by simply pointing out that there are many different interpretations of the United States Constitution (and probably of every set of basic laws in the world), and that diversity of interpretations does not undermine its authority. For US law, the Constitution remains authoritative, which is why striving to interpret it correctly is important. Diverse interpretations of the Bible, some of them equally legitimate and seemingly unresolvable, do not undermine its authority. Its authority is *why* we continue to strive toward a unified, correct interpretation.

So how do liberal Christians view the Bible? No one person speaks for all liberal Christians, so my approach will be to look at prototypical liberal Christian theologians to see if there is some underlying unity in their view of the Bible and, if so, how different it is from traditional, orthodox views of the Bible.

According to Gary Dorrien, one eminent liberal theologian, Borden Parker Bowne (1847–1910), longtime professor of theology at Boston University, did not deny the authority of Scripture but argued that the Bible "contains" the word of God but is not itself the word of God.[2] By that he meant that "the authority of scripture lies in the religious power of its ideas, not in any a priori doctrine of scriptural infallibility."[3] According to liberal Methodist theologian Bowne, Scripture has authority insofar as it communicates truth that does not contradict "the enlightened conscience."[4] That elevates "the enlightened conscience" of a modern person to a level of authority above Scripture; the enlightened conscience then dictates what is and what is not authoritative in Scripture. This set a pattern for many later liberal Christian thinkers to follow. Dorrien says that for early twentieth-century liberal Christians, "the tests of sound theology and discipleship are strictly modern."[5] The Bible was and is subject to the authority of the modernity-shaped enlightened conscience.

2. Gary J. Dorrien, *The Making of American Liberal Theology: Imagining Progressive Religion, 1805–1900* (Louisville: Westminster John Knox, 2001), 382.

3. Ibid., 384.

4. Ibid., 387.

5. Gary J. Dorrien, *The Making of American Liberal Theology: Idealism, Realism, and Modernity, 1900–1950* (Louisville: Westminster John Knox, 2003), 62.

According to Dorrien, another early twentieth-century liberal Protestant thinker, George Burman Foster (1858–1918), who taught theology and philosophy of religion at the University of Chicago Divinity School, "insisted that one cannot be modern and still accept the dualistic supernatural worldview of the Bible."⁶ Notice that he did not mean that the Bible is misunderstood when orthodox Christians base their supernatural worldview on it; he meant that the Bible communicates a supernatural worldview, and that worldview is false. How he or any liberal Christian thinker comes to that conclusion is puzzling. Conservative, orthodox Christians wonder which modern facts falsify the worldview of the Bible. Most liberal Christians would answer, "Science!" But science is simply the study of what is observable by scientific means; what if William Shakespeare was right that "there are more things in heaven and earth, Horatio, than are dreamt of in your philosophy"?⁷ Substitute "science" for "philosophy," and that dramatic question remains relevant to those who limit what's real to what science can discover.

Dorrien ends the second volume of his magisterial three-volume history of American liberal religion by summarizing twentieth-century liberal theology. He repeatedly emphasizes liberal theology's modernist tendencies, its elevation of modern knowledge to the status of controlling authority, although he also claims that liberals reject external authority. This reveals a tension in Dorrien's otherwise superlative history of American liberal religion and theology. On the one hand, he rightly says, liberals all tend to tear down the "house

6. Ibid., 159.
7. Shakespeare, *Hamlet*, act 1, scene 5.

of authority" (meaning external authority, outside the self), while at the same time all treat modern knowledge as external authority. "One way or another, liberal theology always took its stand on the verdicts of modern knowledge and experience without bowing to external authority claims."[8] That means that the Bible could not and cannot function as an authority over modern knowledge even though modern knowledge is changing constantly. Liberal Christianity, therefore, must keep up with the latest trends in modern knowledge and constantly change its beliefs as culture evolves. One thing, however, has remained constant in liberal Christianity since Schleiermacher and that is it "had to dispense with the mythical aspects of Christianity in order to speak the rational language of truth," as truth is defined by the current knowledge of modern culture.[9]

The problem is that for liberal Christians "the mythical aspects of Christianity" include everything miraculous and supernatural. That means that liberal theology has had to demythologize the Bible and Christian tradition to the point of turning Christianity into a pale reflection of the best of secular culture. It allows modern knowledge, whatever that is at the moment, to stand in authority over the Bible even in the most important matters. Of course, what count as the most important matters is a point of major disagreement between orthodox Christians and liberal Christians. Orthodox Christians say, for example, that the bodily resurrection and real return of Jesus Christ to establish his kingdom are among

---

8. Dorrien, *Making of American Liberal Theology: Idealism, Realism, and Modernity*, 534.
9. Ibid.

the most important matters, in both the Bible and Christian tradition. Liberal Christians say that the most important matters have to do with the triumph of spirit over nature—however that is interpreted. Liberal Christians in the twenty-first century most often define the triumph of spirit over nature in terms of liberation from oppression. Conservative, orthodox Christians agree that liberation from oppression is an important theme of the Bible and of Christianity generally, but they will argue that liberation from oppression includes Jesus' resurrection and return.

Throughout this book, I will return repeatedly to liberal theologian Delwin Brown because he expresses the essential ideas of liberal Christianity so concisely and clearly. With some others, it is sometimes difficult to tell exactly what they mean; with Brown that is never the case. In a dialogue with conservative-evangelical theologian Clark Pinnock, Brown said, "To summarize my view, the Bible is not the criterion of truth,"[10] and, "The Bible does not 'norm' us, it does form us.'"[11] What did he mean by "form us"? It shapes our lives; it gives us guidance and direction. But it does not stand in authority over us. Again, Brown declared that the Christian's relationship to the Bible "is not one of being normed by the text, whether in its precise letter or its general spirit, but of being formed by the Bible as we wrestle with its witness."[12] Witness to what? To the "grace of Christ," which is "absolutely the best."[13] But when it comes to believing the truth, Brown said

10. Clark H. Pinnock and Delwin Brown, *Theological Crossfire: An Evangelical/Liberal Dialogue* (Grand Rapids: Zondervan, 1990), 28.
11. Ibid., 29.
12. Ibid., 245.
13. Ibid., 165.

that the Bible is not the criterion. What is? "The best that is known about the rest of the world," which is reconceived in each age.[14] In our age, it is conceived by modern sciences and often, wrongly, as naturalistic.

Historian of liberal theology Kenneth Cauthen, himself a liberal Protestant, expressed the general liberal approach to the Bible clearly. According to him, liberal Christianity views the Bible as "a testimony to the way [the] pioneers of the true faith met, knew, and served God in their own generation."[15] While it awakens and clarifies true spirituality, "its ancient categories must be revised in the light of new knowledge."[16] What ancient categories? All liberal Christian literature makes clear that anything supernatural or miraculous in the Bible is to be doubted, if not denied—except as symbols of spiritual transformation that can happen within a person's (and a society's) soul through the "activation" of the "Christlike Spirit" that shines through them.[17] One can easily read Cauthen's entire history of American religious liberalism without finding any positive mention of the authority of the Bible, except as something liberals want to set aside in favor of religious experiences and the new knowledge of modernity.

Washington Gladden was one of the first outspoken and courageous American liberal theologians and a leader in the social gospel movement. Unlike some later liberal theologians, he did not reject the unique nature of the Bible, but he did

---

14. Ibid., 81, 82, 83.
15. Kenneth Cauthen, *The Impact of American Religious Liberalism*, 2nd ed. (1962; Lanham, MD: Univ. Press of America, 1983), 210.
16. Ibid., 211.
17. Ibid., 210.

call for new interpretations of it based on the new "social consciousness" and "in the light of this century."[18] According to him, interpretations of the Bible must change in light of those cultural changes, but "a wise conservation must always be united with a courageous radicalism."[19] Whether he succeeded in this unification will be decided in later chapters here.

Conservative, orthodox Christians do not reject new interpretations of the Bible insofar as they are based on facts and not cultural preferences and sensitivities. Just because culture changes does not mean biblical interpretation must change. Liberal Christianity is too eager to change interpretation of the Bible to fit current, even secular cultural beliefs and norms. This was evangelical theologian Clark Pinnock's complaint about liberal theology in his dialogue with Delwin Brown. Pinnock stated liberal Christianity's main problem as "its apparent willingness to break with foundational proclamation. . . . It leaves the way open to reduce and distort the Word of God under pressure of modern ideas."[20] Pinnock was orthodox in his basic Christian beliefs about God, Jesus Christ, salvation, and the Bible, but he was willing to reconsider traditional interpretations of the Bible and doctrines in light of hard facts brought out by the sciences. He was also willing to break away from some traditional Christian beliefs when he became convinced that the Bible had been misinterpreted under pressures from, for example, Greek philosophies. However, he did not believe the Bible should

---

18. Washington Gladden, *Present Day Theology* (Columbus, OH: McClelland, 1913), 16, 8.

19. Ibid., 20.

20. Pinnock and Brown, *Theological Crossfire*, 36.

be radically reinterpreted just because contemporary people have trouble believing it.[21]

Henry Churchill King was one of the most influential American liberal theologians around the turn of the nineteenth to the twentieth century. He strongly affirmed the uniqueness and unsurpassability of the Bible, something not typical of liberals.[22] He also affirmed the Bible's "dual authorship" by God and the human prophets and apostles. However, King argued that higher criticism of the Bible required a "restatement of the doctrine of inspiration."[23] With regard to God's authorship of the Bible, King asserted that "God has . . . probably not at any point stepped in miraculously to get a mechanically perfect outcome, when the morally ideal result did not appear. He is not dictating ideal propositions; he is educating men."[24] Conservative, orthodox theologians like Pinnock (and most others) will agree with what King denied (i.e., divine dictation) but disagree with his seeming belief that inspiration amounted only to illumination of the hearts and minds of the human authors. Also, conservative, orthodox theologians will disagree with King's statement that "the Bible . . . may perhaps best be conceived as the record of the preeminent meetings of God with men."[25] It is that, but more. Also, according to King, "We must learn to distinguish in theology between the superficially biblical and the really biblical."[26]

---

21. See Clark H. Pinnock, *The Scripture Principle* (New York: Harper and Row, 1984).

22. Henry Churchill King, *Reconstruction in Theology* (New York: Macmillan, 1901), 165–67.

23. Ibid., 155.

24. Ibid., 161.

25. Ibid., 158.

26. Ibid., 155.

How is the question. By following "the spirit of his [the theologian's] time."[27]

King is best regarded as a mediating theologian—neither wholly liberal nor wholly conservative-orthodox. In his reconstruction of Christian theology, he strove to stay close to traditional, classical, orthodox Christianity, but throughout his book he often strayed away from that into territory determined by modern thought. Although he wanted to have a high view of Scripture, some of what he wrote about it undermined its authority and placed the best of modern culture, philosophy, and science over it. This will be seen when we turn to his reconstructions of the doctrines of God and Christ.

L. Harold DeWolf was also something of a mediating theologian, yet he identified as liberal. He certainly was not as radical in his reconstructions of Christianity in light of modernity as many other liberals. He even said of himself, "The author . . . is not 'liberal' in any meaning of the term as now commonly understood in American theological circles."[28] As was already seen, however, he argued that "the mood and thought of our age" require change in the way we communicate the gospel.[29] He identified two characteristics of the older theology that he considered hindrances to a reasonable communication of the gospel today: biblical literalism and defiance of the natural sciences.[30] For him, modern Christianity must be above all reasonable in modern terms.[31] With regard to the

27. Ibid.
28. L. Harold DeWolf, *The Case for Theology in Liberal Perspective* (Philadelphia: Westminster, 1959), 11.
29. Ibid., 43.
30. Ibid.
31. Ibid., 45.

Bible, DeWolf argued, this requires a cautious "accommodation to culture"[32] that recognizes "the plain fact . . . that the level of truth varies greatly in different parts of the Bible. . . . The writings of the Bible are the writings of men, conditioned and limited by their times and individual peculiarities, though also rising frequently to great heights of expression under the illumination of God's self-disclosing presence. The reader who would hear the true word of God in the reading of the Bible must be prepared to discriminate between the Word of God and the words of men."[33] How does one do that? For DeWolf, in true liberal fashion, modern reason is the key. An example of something he believed was "borderline teaching" within the Bible—not necessary or important for modern Christianity—is the existence of "super-human creatures of God."[34] Without doubt he was referring to angels, Satan, and demons.

To be sure, many modern, secular people are uncomfortable with the idea of "super-human creatures of God" such as angels, Satan, and demons. But is belief in angels, Satan, and demons so irrational? Long after DeWolf virtually denied their existence, in spite of the prominent role they play in the biblical drama, psychologist and author M. Scott Peck (1936–2005) wrote *People of the Lie: The Hope for Healing Human Evil*, expounding his experience-based belief in the demonic as a superhuman power of evil that sometimes is the only explanation for the evil people do.[35] This belief came out of his experiences with clients in therapy, and in the book he even

---

32. Ibid., 58.
33. Ibid., 48.
34. Ibid., 57.
35. M. Scott Peck, *People of the Lie: The Hope for Healing Human Evil* (New York: Simon and Schuster, 1983).

gives case studies of exorcisms in which he participated. When Peck wrote the book, he was a secular psychologist. He became a Christian in part because of his experiences of evil that could not be explained in purely secular terms.

Do DeWolf and other liberal Christians jump the gun when they dismiss whole categories of characters and events in the Bible only because they think those are unbelievable by modernized people? Probably so. One really cannot confess the Bible as God's Word and at the same time deny the reality, however exactly depicted, of superpersonal powers of good and evil in a spiritual realm beyond scientific discovery.

Liberal theologian Donald E. Miller addressed the Bible from the perspective of faith as "troubled commitment."[36] According to him, liberal Christians are persons "in a state of disbelief, struggling for some constructive way to make sense of our experiences."[37] For him, the Bible contains truth within human forms. The human forms are symbols and metaphors and even "social constructions."[38] He distinguished between the form and the substance within the Bible, with the forms being fictional while the substance is or can be real.[39] For him, the substance is "the symbolic form of Jesus."[40] This assertion reveals his confusion. Is Jesus form or substance? Can Miller really distinguish them so clearly? For him, the Bible is "susceptible to all the canons of modern historical and literary analysis" and its authority is always weighed by the authority of reason.[41]

36. Donald E. Miller, *The Case for Liberal Christianity* (San Francisco: Harper and Row, 1981), 23.

37. Ibid., 3.

38. Ibid., 15.

39. Ibid.

40. Ibid., 137.

41. Ibid., 36, 35.

Miller was a proponent of symbolic realism. What really matters to Christianity, he avers, is "the mystery of the Christian experience . . . that there is a Reality that stands both within and beyond our humanly created symbols."[42] The Bible, then, consists of humanly created symbols pointing to "Reality." All of our conceptions of that reality, even those found in the Bible, are "fictive" in nature, only "representations of the Holy." Miller falls into contradiction with himself again when he says, "Reality is always a social construction."[43] Apparently nothing is *not* a social construction. What, then, of the distinction between form and substance? Ultimately, even the substance is fictive. What Christianity is actually about remains amazingly vague, except that it is "a common symbolic paradigm."[44] And the Bible's only significance is that it gives rise to that paradigm. In the final analysis, Miller confesses that his faith is "beliefless obedience."[45] But obedience to what? And why? How is the Bible different for Miller from *The Lord of the Rings*? Untold millions of young people around the world find that classic fantasy epic to be the fountain of their symbolic universe that gives rise to their obedience to a certain way of life. Why regard the Bible as better, more authoritative, than any other book?

If you think I am misrepresenting Miller, consider again these statements from his book *The Case for Liberal Christianity*: "I have given up on trying to settle the question of the resurrection, whether Jesus was born of a virgin, whether

---

42. Ibid., 20.
43. Ibid., 6.
44. Ibid., 10.
45. Ibid., 4.

he made the blind see and the lame walk."[46] "I presently feel comfortable reciting the creed without editing it or feeling a pang of conscience if I affirm something that I do not literally believe."[47] Years ago I saw a book titled *I Have Abandoned My Search for Truth and Am Now Looking for a Good Fantasy* by self-help guru Ashleigh Brilliant.[48] Miller could say he has found a good fantasy—his liberal Christianity.

Marcus Borg was a leading member of the Jesus Seminar, a collective of higher critics of the Bible, especially the New Testament gospels, who were searching for the historical Jesus. In *The God We Never Knew*, Borg promotes higher criticism of the Gospels and claims that "statements [in the Gospels] in which Jesus affirms an exalted status for himself are not found in the earliest layers" of the oral and written traditions behind the Gospels.[49] For him, and for most liberal Christians, the Gospels are products of traditions handed down through the first and second centuries, and therefore they cannot be considered reliable sources for what Jesus really said or did. Much of what the Gospels record and report as sayings of Jesus are simply sayings of later Christian prophets, for example, claiming to speak on behalf of Jesus. Or the sayings are simply myths developed in ancient Christian circles to exalt Jesus to divine status.[50] Higher criticism allegedly reveals that "Jesus did not speak of himself (and apparently did not think of himself) as

46. Ibid., 5.
47. Ibid.
48. Ashleigh Brilliant, *I Have Abandoned My Search for Truth and Am Now Looking for a Good Fantasy* (Brilliant Enterprises, 1981).
49. Marcus J. Borg, *The God We Never Knew: Beyond Dogmatic Religion to a More Authentic Contemporary Faith* (New York: HarperCollins, 1997), 88.
50. Ibid., 88, 102.

divine."[51] Jesus' virgin birth and resurrection are myths, and his death was simply a martyrdom.[52]

Clearly, Borg does not consider the Bible true in any historical sense. Presumably, then, he would agree with Miller that the Bible is a fountain of symbols and images that express experiences of God. What experiences of God? "The Christian life is about turning toward and entering into relationship with the one who is already in relationship with us," Borg says.[53]

Perhaps no recent liberal theologian has been as radical in his rejection of traditional Christian beliefs about the Bible as John Shelby Spong. For the late Episcopal bishop, "The Bible is not the word of God in any literal or verbal sense. It never has been!"[54] What is important to Christianity, he wrote in *Why Christianity Must Change or Die*, is "the Jesus experience," which needs to be separated from the New Testament and the doctrinal developments of the church.[55] For him, everything in the New Testament (he hardly bothers with the Old Testament!) is historical-mythical interpretation developed within the first-century churches from their experiences of the sacred through their encounter with Jesus Christ. But even what the New Testament says about Jesus is more mythical than historical. Spong throws into that category Jesus' resurrection and his preexistence as the Son of God in heaven.[56]

So what remains of the New Testament for Spong? For him the Gospels are "treasured biblical tales" and "history . . .

---

51. Ibid., 88.
52. Ibid., 101–2.
53. Ibid., 79.
54. John Shelby Spong, *Why Christianity Must Change or Die: A Bishop Speaks to Believers in Exile* (San Francisco: HarperSanFrancisco, 1998), 72.
55. Ibid., 73.
56. Ibid., 80.

interpreted in rather dramatic and fanciful ways."[57] How does he know this? Simply because of "the way life is now understood," "the light of contemporary understandings of the world."[58] Again, a liberal Christian elevates modern thought to the status of an authority above the Bible, and *modern thought* is interpreted by him as requiring a naturalistic understanding of reality. Of course, this, too, could be merely a passing form of humanity.

At the end of this tour of liberal Christianity's accounts of the Bible, our honest conclusion must be that it has cut the cord of continuity between itself and classical, orthodox Christianity so fully and finally that what is left is unrecognizable as authentically Christian. Orthodox Christians may never fully agree on the details of the Bible, the relationship between the Bible and tradition, or the interpretation of obscure passages of the Bible, but we have always agreed that the Bible is God's Word written, supernaturally inspired and authoritative over fads and cultural trends.

---

57. Ibid., 15.
58. Ibid., 16, 19.

CHAPTER 4

GOD ACCORDING TO LIBERAL THEOLOGY

Revising the traditional Christian doctrine of God has been a major project of modern liberal Christian theology. Probably no single subject has consumed so much attention in the literature of liberal theology. This subject includes divine action and especially miracles. The majority of liberal Christian thinkers do not believe in supernatural divine interventions in nature or history. However, the revisions go deeper. Most modern liberal Christian thinkers oppose the idea of a transcendent, sovereign, personal deity like the one classical, orthodox Christianity teaches and worships.

Some critics will attempt to argue that Christians have always disagreed about God, that there has always been more diversity of opinion about God than uniform belief. True, Christians have long debated details about the doctrine of God.[1] There is no point in hiding the fact that orthodox Christians have long disagreed about secondary matters such as the exact nature of God's relationship with time, God's immutability (changelessness), the exact extent of God's power, and the inner "workings" of the Trinity. However, underlying those disagreements exists a consensus about God. According to traditional Christianity, on the basis of the biblical witness and reason, God is absolute in the sense of being unconditioned by anything outside himself. God may limit his power, but nothing outside God limits God's power. God intervenes in nature and history with acts commonly called miracles—events that can never be explained naturally. God is the creator of all that exists outside himself, having created the universe out of nothing. These and many more unifying concepts of God have provided significant unity amid the diversity of Christian beliefs about God throughout the centuries, up until the emergence of the modern, secular worldview.

Before the first liberal theologian, Friedrich Schleiermacher, many free-thinking skeptics such as the deists and philosopher David Hume (1711–76), who was an agnostic, if not an atheist, questioned and cast aspersions on orthodox Christian beliefs about God, especially miracles. Early Unitarians questioned the Trinity and grew to doubt miracles. But Schleiermacher was the first mainline Protestant minister-theologian openly to deny miracles such as Jesus' bodily resurrection (and get away with it). Schleiermacher opened the floodgates of liberal-modernist

---

1. Again, I recommend my book *The Mosaic of Christian Belief: Twenty Centuries of Unity and Diversity*, 2nd ed. (Downers Grove, IL: InterVarsity Press, 2016), especially its chapters on God.

thinking among Protestants first in Europe and then in America and around the world.

A handy label for orthodox Christian belief about God is *Christian theism*. I will use that phrase to signal traditional, biblical-orthodox Christian belief about God. The basic contours of Christian theism include that God is transcendent and immanent, holy love, self-sufficient, sovereign (even if limiting his control over free creatures' decisions and actions), ultimately and finally real—being itself, the source and ground of all being, all-wise and faithful. Also, God is omnipotent (some prefer the term *almighty*), omniscient, and omnipresent— the three "omnis" of classical Christian theism. Finally, for now, God cares and intervenes both in nature and history with acts of power and love and justice that transcend any natural explanation. Miracles are not, as Hume called them, "violations" of natural laws; they are, as C. S. Lewis explained in *Miracles*, suspensions of the normal operations of natural laws.[2] According to classical, orthodox Christian thought, natural laws are not ironclad laws separate from God, parts of a great cosmic machine that exists over against God, but operations of God's general providence. Therefore, suspending one or more is not the same as violating them. God does not have to break into nature to act miraculously or supernaturally. He simply suspends the ordinary working of his own operations to make a miracle happen.

Somehow a spell has fallen over modernist-liberal Christian minds, making them think that modern science somehow excludes miracles, special interventions of God in

---

2. C. S. Lewis, *Miracles* (New York: Macmillan, 1947).

nature and history. Most liberal Christians think that one has to choose between being scientifically minded and believing in classical theism. That simply is not the case, as Christian theologian Horace Bushnell (1802–76) argued cogently in *Nature and the Supernatural*.[3] The irony here is that Gary Dorrien and other expositors of liberal Christianity typically include Bushnell as the outstanding example of an American liberal Christian minister-theologian. While Bushnell did revise some traditional doctrines such as the atonement, he was not a typical liberal theologian. Against the rising tide of Unitarianism and liberal Protestantism in America and Europe, he staunchly defended belief in miracles while also embracing the advances of modern science.[4]

In this chapter, I will cite several major modernist-liberal Christian thinkers and offer a few of their thoughts about God that demonstrate their cutting the cord of continuity with biblical-orthodox Christianity. In each case, I will mention their ideas about miracles, showing how they effectively deny them. Wherever appropriate, I will mention their beliefs about the Trinity. A whole book could be written about liberal Christian revisions to the doctrine of God; here I will have to abbreviate considerably.

According to Dorrien, liberal Christianity in America

---

3. Horace Bushnell, *Nature and the Supernatural* (New York: Scribner, 1858).

4. Gary Dorrien is ambivalent about Bushnell and his legacy. See chapter 3 of Gary Dorrien, *The Making of American Liberal Theology: Imagining Progressive Religion, 1805–1900* (Louisville: Westminster John Knox, 2001), 111–78—the longest single chapter devoted to an individual in Dorrien's three-volume set. On the one hand, Dorrien treats Bushnell as the most important and influential American liberal theologian of the nineteenth century. On the other hand, he admits that Bushnell really did not fit the profile of a liberal theologian, labeling his theology "progressive orthodoxy."

arose from a desire to discover a "third way" between the authority-based orthodoxies of traditional Christianity and the "spiritless materialism of modern atheism/deism."[5] One impetus for such a discovery was the romanticism of Christian thinkers such as Samuel Taylor Coleridge (1772–1834) and Ralph Waldo Emerson (1803–82). Coleridge was an orthodox Christian, but he emphasized the immanence of God, as all liberal Christians have and do. Emerson was a Unitarian, but one who objected to rationalism in religion and emphasized feeling and interpreted God as the "Oversoul" of the universe (a view of God badly labeled *transcendentalism*). Likewise, Schleiermacher was a romanticist who emphasized the human relationship with God as feeling (*Gefühl*). He strongly encouraged belief in God's transcendence while at the same time promoting belief in God's immanence in a new and unorthodox way. Critics often accused him of pantheism—a false accusation, yet an idea that could easily arise from his emphasis on God's immanence within humanity.

Eventually, liberal Christians settled on panentheism as the third way. Panentheism is the idea that God and the world are interdependent, that God did not create the universe out of nothing, that God is immanent in the world and the world is immanent in God. This began formally with German philosopher-theologian Georg Wilhelm Friedrich Hegel (1770–1831), who considered himself a Protestant Christian but radically revised the doctrine of God, labeling God the "Absolute Spirit" and describing God as actualizing himself in and through human history. Some version of this

---

5. Ibid., xiii.

panentheistic understanding of God worked its way into liberal Protestant theology in Europe and America in the nineteenth and twentieth centuries, and panentheism became the accepted third way Dorrien mentioned.

According to influential historians Cauthen and Hutchison, liberal Christianity's essence includes a new idea of and a new emphasis on God's immanence. That emphasis, however, does not translate into belief in God's special providence in miraculous interventions. According to Cauthen, liberal theology is marked by "a dominant liberal worldview" that he labels "monism."[6] Cauthen explains, "In short, the universe is a unified, dynamic process activated by an immanent Christlike Spirit whose supreme goal is the establishment of a kingdom of love and brotherhood on earth."[7] "No special, miraculous revelations are necessary."[8] For most liberal Christians, God is that "immanent Christlike Spirit." What is missing is the orthodox belief in God's transcendence.

Hutchison agrees with Cauthen about this dominant liberal worldview pervading liberal Christian thought. Throughout *The Modernist Impulse in American Protestantism*, he refers to the theme of God's immanence as part of the foundation of modernist-liberal theology. For him, divine immanence is one of the three enduring modernist ideas defining liberal Christianity.[9]

Liberal pastor-theologian Washington Gladden referred

6. Kenneth Cauthen, *The Impact of American Religious Liberalism*, 2nd ed. (1962; Lanham, MD: Univ. Press of America, 1983), 209.

7. Ibid., 210.

8. Ibid.

9. William R. Hutchison, *The Modernist Impulse in American Protestantism* (1976; New York and Oxford: Oxford Univ. Press, 1982), 311.

to the immanence of God as "the one ruling conception in present day theology."[10] According to Gladden, "The idea of the immanence of God; the idea that God's method of creation is the method of evolution; the idea that nature in all its deepest meanings is supernatural; the idea of the constant presence of God in our lives; the idea of the universal divine Fatherhood and of the universal human Brotherhood, with all that they imply—these are ideas which are here to stay."[11] To be fair, Gladden did not deny miracles; he sought to define them as "the working out of some law not yet discovered, some deeper and diviner principle of life whose operation is yet to be revealed."[12] Yet, at the same time, he affirmed the uniformity of natural law as "our modern way of looking at things."[13] There is some tension between these concepts that Gladden did not work out.

The problem with Gladden's and other liberal theologians' view of God is not what they affirm but what they deny and why they deny it. An affirmation of the immanence of God is not a problem for orthodox Christianity. Although Gladden seemed to affirm miracles, he also seemed to deny divine interventions, reducing miracles to natural events with causes not yet understood. He rejected "the ruling conception of God as Sovereign, Ruler, Moral Governor" in favor of "the ruling conception of God as Father."[14] And he believed this because of modern "historical consciousness"

---

10. Washington Gladden, *Present Day Theology* (Columbus, OH: McClelland, 1913), 13.

11. Ibid., 6–7.

12. Ibid., 45.

13. Ibid., 44.

14. Ibid., 29.

and "social consciousness." "Our thoughts about God will be modified by these ideas; our explanations of his relations to us will be affected by them."[15] Again, the fatherhood of God is not the problem; the problem is denial of God as sovereign ruler and moral governor.

Henry Churchill King lived and wrote books like *Reconstruction in Theology* around the same time as Gladden, during the heyday of liberal Protestantism in America. Around the turn of the twentieth century, these ideas were new and fresh and exciting; many people regarded liberal Christianity as a liberation from constricting concepts of God that conflicted with modern sensibilities about nature and humanity. According to King, "Theology must grow as science grows."[16] Theology must be reconstructed because of widespread dissatisfaction with traditional doctrinal statements and formulations.[17] King could be considered a mediating theologian insofar as he strove to do justice to "certain convictions of our own day" that call for "a rewriting of theology—a new theology"[18] while at the same time preserving the transcendence of God[19] and miracles. However, like Gladden and other liberal theologians, King promoted an "increased emphasis on the immanence of God,"[20] going so far as to affirm the existence of "an unknown Infinite, as alone giving real causal connection" to all events in

---

15. Ibid., 17.
16. Henry Churchill King, *Reconstruction in Theology* (New York: Macmillan, 1901), 2.
17. Ibid., 15–20. This is my condensed paraphrase of what King argues in these pages.
18. Ibid., 29.
19. Ibid., 108.
20. Ibid., 86.

82

nature.[21] Also like Gladden, King strove to hold on to miracles, but only as unusual acts of God that accord with natural law. If a miracle occurs, the liberal Christian should regard it as God's "loving adaptation of his actions in nature" rather than as any intervention of God in the workings of nature.

Like Gladden, what King affirmed is not so much the problem for orthodox Christians as what he denied. Implicit in his affirmation of "the universality of law" is a denial of God's transcendent interventions in ways science could never explain. He claimed, "God will always act according to law—that is, in perfect consistency with his unchanging purpose of love; but his action may not always be formulable under any of the laws of nature known to us."[22] The implication is that some law of nature can explain any given miracle, even if that law of nature is not yet known to us. This seems to lock God into nature and is driven by the belief in science's alleged discovery of "the universality of law."[23]

A better approach would be to affirm, alongside Bushnell and Lewis, that the laws of nature are human perceptions of the regularities of God's general providence, but sometimes God acts in extraordinary ways not controlled by any natural law. The biblical witness is filled with such events, including the resurrection of Jesus Christ. What law could possibly ever explain that? Jesus' resurrection was not a mere resuscitation of a corpse; he had taken on a new kind of life fit for heaven. The resurrection transcends any law conceivably discoverable by science. Both Gladden and King should be commended for

21. Ibid., 103.
22. Ibid., 61.
23. Ibid., 56.

attempting to integrate Christianity with modern science and vice versa, but they both fell short by succumbing to the idea that even God must operate like nature operates—according to laws. This puts the concept of law over God rather than God over law.

Orthodox Christianity has no problem with God's obeying laws that are part of his character; God has an eternal, unchanging character that governs (not controls) his actions. For example, God cannot lie; God cannot break promises. That is because God is truth and faithfulness. The problem with King's proposal is that it attempts to impose a quasi-scientific concept of law, as in "laws of nature," on God. For King, the known laws of nature are simply broadened to include the unknown laws of nature, both of which limit God's activity. Whether King intended that is unclear; perhaps he did not. However, if he did not, he should have been more cautious in his language about God always working according to laws. Based on the biblical story and witness, God stands above all laws except those of his own nature, and he does intervene in the ordinary operations of nature in ways that transcend the laws discoverable by human beings.

L. Harold DeWolf stands out from the crowd of liberal Christian thinkers as an exception in his conception of God. He affirmed an orthodox doctrine of God, including God's special providence—divine acts that transcend scientific reason and law.[24] That is not to say DeWolf embraced irrationalism; he did not. He emphasized reason in theology but saw no reason why special, intervening acts of God should be irrational

---

24. L. Harold DeWolf, *The Case for Theology in Liberal Perspective* (Philadelphia: Westminster, 1959), 85.

insofar as God is a part of the worldview. DeWolf's Christology is not orthodox, as I will show in the next chapter, but he affirmed the Trinity, which seems inconsistent with his doctrine of the person of Jesus Christ. (This distinction will be explained in chapter 5.) DeWolf's doctrine of the Trinity suffers from some inconsistencies. He often refers to Father, Son, and Holy Spirit as "modes of God's revelation" yet also treats them as distinct persons—contradicting Unitarianism, deism, and transcendentalism.[25]

Like many liberal Christians, DeWolf was shockingly inconsistent. He affirmed special divine acts of special providence (miracles), but he questioned the literal truth of the virgin birth of Jesus Christ and the resurrection.[26] Sometimes he seemed, at least in *The Case for Theology in Liberal Perspective*, to want to have his cake and eat it, too. He struggled to hold on to the gospel while demythologizing biblical events such as the second coming of Jesus Christ.[27] His liberal colors will come more clearly into focus in later chapters, but he must be given credit for at least trying to avoid the radical revisioning of Christianity into which some liberal thinkers have fallen.

Liberal theologian Delwin Brown, in his dialogue with conservative theologian Clark Pinnock, argued that God must be reconceived in each age.[28] "To be defensible, liberal Christians assume, a concept of God must be consistent with

---

25. Ibid., 110–14.
26. Ibid., 74–82.
27. Ibid., 179.
28. Clark H. Pinnock and Delwin Brown, *Theological Crossfire: An Evangelical/Liberal Dialogue* (Grand Rapids: Zondervan, 1990), 82–83.

the best that is known about the rest of the world."[29] Again, as Pinnock points out, this is not in and of itself wrong. The key debatable point lies in the word "known." What is believed to be known about the world changes all the time and never undermines the basic truths Christianity proclaims about God. Cultural ideas may undermine basic Christian truths, but those ideas cannot claim to be knowledge that undermines belief in God or God's self-revelation. The two are on different planes. What Brown and most other liberals claim as "the best that is known about the rest of the world" often turns out to be ephemeral cultural concepts of reality.

Brown's problem appears when he goes on to claim that modern Christians must believe that God and the world are interdependent (which is known as panentheism).[30] "God's being is intertwined with that of the world."[31] This is Brown's liberal expression of God's immanence, and it leads him to deny God's omnipotence.[32] One has to wonder, as Pinnock does, how any modern knowledge about reality can require such conclusions. Brown is an adherent of a particular type of liberal theology known as process theology, which stems from the philosophy of Alfred North Whitehead (1861–1947). Process philosophy and theology include belief in God's essential limitations and "becoming" in relation to ever-changing world reality. This is highly speculative and unprovable. And it conflicts profoundly with orthodox Christianity. What is its purpose and value? Not that it fits the best of knowledge

29. Ibid., 81.
30. Ibid., 85.
31. Ibid., 87.
32. Ibid., 86.

about the world but that it allegedly solves the problem of evil. If God is ever becoming and not omnipotent, then God is not responsible for the evil and innocent suffering in the world. This idea is attractive to many people after the genocidal twentieth century, but it comes at the expense of confidence in any future victory of good over evil. As one critic said, the only thing wrong with process theology is that it is such an attractive alternative to Christianity. Brown does not seem to understand that.

Donald E. Miller presents one of the most radical versions of liberal Christianity in *The Case for Liberal Christianity*. For him, as for many liberal Christian thinkers, "God is synonymous with the search for human wholeness, for confidence in the ultimate meaningfulness of human existence."[33] God is, Miller claims, "the life-force."[34] These two statements hardly cohere. Which is it? Is God the search and the confidence, or is God the life force? Or is God both? Miller fails to explain how God is or could be both. Saying that God is "the search for" seems inconsistent with a metaphysical claim about God's immanence as the "life-force." In either case, Miller's God is not the God of orthodox-biblical Christianity.

Like Brown, Miller claims that liberal Christianity's revisions of classical Christian doctrines are based on the attempt "to understand God . . . in terms of the best available scientific knowledge and social analysis."[35] But how do scientific knowledge and/or social analysis yield a requirement to revise the

33. Donald E. Miller, *The Case for Liberal Christianity* (San Francisco: Harper and Row, 1981), 37.
34. Ibid., 38.
35. Ibid., 33.

doctrine of God? They don't—unless naturalism is smuggled into them, which it often wrongly is.[36]

Peter Hodgson echoes Brown and other liberal process theologians when, in *Liberal Theology: A Radical Vision*, he writes that "God is not a static, transcendent beyond but is becoming God through interaction with and embodiment in the world."[37] That is a concise statement of process theology and a mere assertion; it cannot be demonstrated by Scripture, tradition, reason, or experience. Actually, though, Hodgson appeals to German philosopher Hegel, who wrote long before the rise of process theology. For Hodgson and Hegel, God should be understood as "evolving Spirit."[38] To be fair, Hodgson, like most process thinkers, affirms God as free and personal, but also like most (or all) process thinkers, he entangles God so deeply with the world and its processes that God loses the power to overcome evil. Hodgson's view of God is an example of panentheism—the idea going back at least to Hegel that God and the world are interdependent. Hegel famously said, "Without a world, God is not God."[39] Hodgson echoes this when he writes, "History is not . . . a sideshow but constitutive of the divine life,"[40] and, "God actualizes godself in and through the world."[41]

---

36. For a devastating critique demonstrating how naturalism is not only not required by science but actually undermines science, see Alvin Plantinga, *Where the Conflict Really Lies: Science, Religion, and Naturalism* (New York: Oxford Univ. Press, 2011).

37. Peter Crafts Hodgson, *Liberal Theology: A Radical Vision* (Minneapolis: Fortress, 2007), 22.

38. Ibid., 37.

39. Quoted in Quentin Lauer, *Hegel's Concept of God* (Albany, NY: State Univ. of New York Press, 1982), 79.

40. Hodgson, *Liberal Theology*, 43.

41. Ibid., 45.

Hodgson even goes so far as to deny that the Holy Spirit or any persons of the Trinity preexisted history. "The Holy Spirit is not something that exists in advance as a supernatural person of the godhead. There are no such preexisting persons in God but rather potentials for relationships that become actual when God creates the world."[42] This affirmation that God creates the world seems inconsistent with Hodgson's claim that "the inner-trinitarian relationships take on the character of personal subjects only in relation to the world."[43] Frankly, I cannot make any sense of these conflicting ideas. How could God create the world if God is not actual prior to the world's coming into existence and if God becomes personal only in relation to the world?

Orthodox-biblical Christianity depends on belief in the prior actuality of God. God is fully actual before the world comes into existence, and the world can come into existence only because God precedes it with full actuality of being. That is not to say that God cannot have new experiences in relation to the world. The biblical narrative indicates that he does. But God does not depend on the world for his being fully and perfectly God. Hodgson's panentheism is such a step away from orthodox Christianity's consensus about God that it really cannot be considered authentically Christian.

Liberal theologian Marcus Borg is right to assert, "How we think about God matters."[44] However, in his book *The God We Never Knew*, he strongly recommends panentheism as the best

42. Ibid., 39.
43. Ibid., 40.
44. Marcus J. Borg, *The God We Never Knew: Beyond Dogmatic Religion to a More Authentic Contemporary Faith* (New York: HarperCollins, 1997), vii.

way to rethink God in contemporary culture.[45] He recounts
in some detail his childhood and youthful "pictures" of God
developed from church experiences. Apparently, he was led to
believe in a distant, remote, totally transcendent God. Later
in life, as a trained New Testament scholar, he began to think
of God as more immanent than transcendent. Of course, he
argues that panentheism balances God's immanence and
transcendence. However, he came to reject what he calls
"supernatural theism" in favor of seeing God as "encompassing
spirit." He claims, "In our time, thinking of God as a supernatural being 'out there' has become an obstacle for many."[46]
Under the influence of the modern worldview, Borg embraced
and promoted a panentheistic view of God as transcendent
and immanent, but a reader of his book cannot be blamed
for thinking that he allowed the transcendence of God to fall
away in favor of a totally immanent God.

At the heart of Borg's revisioning of God is his interest
in finding a relational understanding of the Christian life.[47]
For him, anyway, panentheism is the best way to get there.
An orthodox Christian will not object to a relational understanding of the Christian life; orthodox Christians have always
believed in experiencing God. Again, as with other liberal
Christian thinkers we have encountered, the problem lies not
so much in what Borg affirms as in what he denies. He affirms
a relational God, a God who relates to us and to whom we can
relate. That is not a problem. The trouble lies in his rejection
of supernatural theism. He calls himself an atheist regard-

45. Ibid., 4.
46. Ibid., 12.
47. Ibid., 51.

ing the God of supernatural theism "and yet a believer in God conceptualized another way, namely in the way offered by panentheism."[48]

For Borg, God as "monarch" is rejected while God as "journey companion" is embraced.[49] Yet there is no reason the two concepts must be set against each other. The God of the Bible and of Christian tradition is, indeed, our journey companion insofar as he is intimate with us. Christian church fathers, philosophers, theologians, biblical scholars, and mystics have always affirmed the ideal of intimacy with God. The God who is intimate with us, our journey companion, can also be the ruler of heaven and earth. That seems paradoxical to us only because we have been conditioned by culture to think the two images are contradictory. There is no reason they must be. The Bible reveals God as both exalted, high, lifted up (see Isaiah's vision of God in chapter 6) *and* nearer to each one of us than we are to ourselves (see Saint Augustine's *Confessions*). The Bible is full of images of God's nearness and intimacy with persons. Psalm 139 affirms that the person cannot escape God's presence.

Borg's liberalism appears in what he denies—supernatural theism. However, the God of the Bible, the God of orthodox Christianity, is more than "the encompassing Spirit both within us and outside us."[50] He is the creator and ruler of all things and the judge of people and nations. Yes, he is love itself, the standard of goodness and love, but his love is *holy* love that does not indulge sin. God's wrath is evident in Scripture and Christian tradition—until the emergence of modernist-liberal

---

48. Ibid., 29.
49. Ibid., 75.
50. Ibid., 72.

Christianity. Suddenly, God became Whitehead's "fellow sufferer who understands" and Borg's "journey companion." God is certainly those, but he is also much more.

Of all the liberal Christian thinkers and communicators we have encountered on this journey, the most vehement in rejecting Christian tradition is John Shelby Spong. Spong rejected "the almighty quality of God" and dismissed "most of the God content of the ages."[51] According to Spong, the God of theism is merely a projection that is now dying[52] and that must be replaced by God as a "depth dimension to life that is ultimately spiritual."[53] God, he says, is not external to (creaturely) life but "the inescapable depth and center of all that is."[54] Then, like Hodgson, Spong falls into contradiction by defining God as "a call into being."[55] Which is God: an inescapable depth and center of all that is, or a call into being? Or somehow both? Spong doesn't explain. For no good reason, Spong sacrifices both God's transcendence and God's personhood. God, for him as for many liberal Christians, becomes a "call" and a "depth dimension" with whom one cannot have a personal relationship and who does not love or rule. This picture looks nothing like the God of the Bible or of orthodox Christianity.[56]

Throughout this book, I represent Douglas Ottati as the other bookend on the shelf of liberal theologies, the

---

51. John Shelby Spong, *Why Christianity Must Change or Die: A Bishop Speaks to Believers in Exile* (San Francisco: HarperSanFrancisco, 1998), 8, 48.

52. Ibid., 49, 51.

53. Ibid., 60.

54. Ibid., 70.

55. Ibid., 66.

56. See my book *Essentials of Christian Thought: Seeing Reality through the Biblical Story* (Grand Rapids: Zondervan, 2017). There I plumb the depths of the biblical drama to show that the God of the Bible is ultimately real, ultimately personal, ultimately supernatural (beyond nature as well as within it), and both loving and just.

counterpart to Schleiermacher. Schleiermacher launched the tradition; Ottati is his most faithful contemporary follower (which is not to say he merely repeats what Schleiermacher said). Ottati's *A Theology for the Twenty-First Century* stands as the most profound restatement of Schleiermacher's liberal Christianity. People who wonder whether liberal Christian theology is still a viable type of theology ought to read it. At 770 pages, the book can be a daunting read, but for those interested in theology, reading it is worth the time and effort. The question is, Is Ottati's study about authentic Christianity, or is it a study in comparative religions? Does Ottati really offer *Christianity* for the twenty-first century, or does he cross the line into non-Christian territory?

Ottati's doctrine of God tells part of the story and reveals part of the answer. According to Ottati, who agrees with liberal theologian Gordon Kaufman (1925–2011), "The word 'God' can express 'the profound meaning of the situatedness of human life in the world.'"[57] However, Ottati understands that situation or context "somewhat differently (and significantly) than he does."[58] According to Ottati, God is "source (and ground)" of the human person's "sensed dependence, incompleteness, mystery."[59] God is also "ordering power" behind the "dynamic and dependable arrangements, tendencies, interdependencies, and trajectories that we encounter in the world."[60] God is, "if you like," "the really Real."[61] "God" is a symbol of the "Creator"

---

57. Douglas F. Ottati, *A Theology for the Twenty-First Century* (Grand Rapids: Eerdmans, 2020), 323.

58. Ibid.

59. Ibid., 300.

60. Ibid.

61. Ibid., 302.

and "Sustainer,"[62] but Ottati interprets these through process theology, which "portrays God as the preeminent creative principle who lures or persuades realities that retain their own relatively independent . . . measures of creativity."[63] "The divine creative ordering . . . encourages, discourages, directs, limits, and calls forth."[64] Left unclear in Ottati's symbolic account of God are God's personal nature and the reality of miracles. His endorsement of a "nonreductive naturalism" seems to settle the question of miracles with a no. His emphasis on God as symbol seems to settle the question of God's personal nature with another no. At least so it seems for Ottati, God is not personal in any sense in which humans are personal.

Like Schleiermacher in *The Christian Faith*, Ottati relegates the doctrine of the Trinity to an appendix or epilogue. For him, as for the father of liberal theology, the persons of the Trinity are "three aspects of piety's experience" of God,[65] and he denies or is agnostic about three distinctions within the Godhead.[66] The best that can be said about Ottati's position is that it echoes modalism—the ancient heresy that Father, Son, and Holy Spirit are three manifestations of God and not three distinct persons of the Godhead.

According to Ottati, theology is not as much about doctrines as it is about piety—practical Christianity in lived experience and behavior. Ottati's theology is an example of what theologian George Lindbeck (1923–2018) called

---

62. Ibid., 328.
63. Ibid., 307.
64. Ibid., 313.
65. Ibid., 748.
66. Ibid., 749.

"experiential-expressivist" theology.[67] It expresses religious and Christian feelings, experiences, and sensibilities, but it does not explain anything cognitively or propositionally. Christian doctrines, such as the doctrine of God, then become attempts to bring religious experiences to speech, but those doctrines are not essential for Christianity. Christianity is, Ottati says, "theocentric piety," and Christian theology is "piety teaching."[68] Theology is useful only as a tool for spiritual formation and Christian living; it does not actually inform us cognitively of things-in-themselves. Talk about God, Ottati says, agreeing with Schleiermacher, is never talk about God-in-himself but only talk about our feelings when we encounter God indirectly, which is the only way we encounter God.[69]

The problem with Ottati's doctrine of God, as with all liberal theological talk about God, at least according to orthodox Christianity, is not so much what it affirms as what it implicitly or explicitly denies—God's transcendent reality, God's intensely and supremely personal nature, God's self-communication to us in real historical acts of power and love, God's triune being as Father, Son, and Holy Spirit, three distinct persons in perfect community. One thing liberal Christianity implicitly denies that orthodox Christianity has always affirmed is God's creation of the whole universe *ex nihilo*—out of nothing.[70] Ottati treats that as a helpful symbol of God's ordering of things in the universe, but he seems

67. George A. Lindbeck, *The Nature of Doctrine: Religion and Theology in a Postliberal Age* (1984; Louisville: Westminster John Knox, 2009).
68. Ottati, *A Theology for the Twenty-First Century*, 581.
69. Ibid., 296.
70. Ibid., 307.

to prefer the "alternative doctrine" of process theology, which denies creation out of nothing.[71]

In the middle of the twentieth century, Christian theologian H. Richard Niebuhr, himself something of a theological liberal (at least according to Dorrien), leveled the harshest criticism of liberal Protestantism. Niebuhr's criticism applies to all of the liberal thinkers discussed in this book. According to him, liberal Christianity believes "a God without wrath brought men without sin into a kingdom without judgment through the ministrations of a Christ without a cross."[72] Of course, none of them actually denies that Christ died on a Roman cross; what Niebuhr meant was that the liberals denied Christ's atoning death, reducing it to a tragic martyrdom.

The question we are wrestling with in this book is whether liberal Christianity counts as authentic Christianity or as a new and different religion, something other than Christianity. These liberal theologians' accounts of God should make the answer to that question clear. The God of liberal Christianity is nothing like the God of the Abraham, Isaac, and Jacob, or Jesus. French mathematician, philosopher, and theologian Blaise Pascal (1623–62) said, "The God of the philosophers is not the God of Abraham, Isaac, and Jacob." By "the philosophers," he meant not only Enlightenment thinkers like René

---

71. Ottati can be frustratingly ambiguous at times. An example is his treatment of the traditional Christian doctrine of creation *ex nihilo*. On pages 305–17 of *A Theology for the Twenty-First Century*, he wrestles with it, pointing out its strengths and weaknesses, and eventually seems to side with process theology against it. However, he also seems to value it as a symbol of God's supreme creativity, as "cosmic passage."

72. H. Richard Niebuhr, *The Kingdom of God in America* (Chicago: Willett, Clark, 1937), 193.

Descartes (1596–1650) but also others such as Greek philosophers Plato and Aristotle. Why? Because they could not conceive of God rationally as personal, supernatural, intimate, interactive, transcendent, and immanent.

The question has to be raised *why* these liberal theologians found and find it necessary to empty God of his transcendence, almighty power, self-sufficiency, personhood (in some cases), and wrath. Historian William Hutchison suggests an answer. According to him, liberal theologians sought "somehow to inject a new self-esteem into the human historical consciousness."[73] Ironically, Spong's critique of supernatural theism as projection can easily be turned around; it may be Spong's and other liberals' ideas of God that are projections of the human need for self-esteem onto ultimate reality, calling that *God*. A major question is whether this God is worthy of worship. The orthodox God of Christian theism is worthy of worship because he is both and equally great and good. Liberal theology sacrifices God's greatness, and we are left with a pathetic God who seems more like a nice, heavenly grandfather or a deep, spiritual dimension of man (or nature) than the God of the Bible.

---

73. Hutchison, *Modernist Impulse in American Protestantism*, 80.

CHAPTER 5

JESUS CHRIST IN
LIBERAL THEOLOGY

If there is one Christian doctrine that stands out as especially defining Christian orthodoxy, it is of the person of Jesus Christ, his incarnation, his being not only the Son of God but also God the Son. Of course, anyone who has studied church history knows there have been many disagreements and quarrels among Christians about this doctrine. Historian Philip Jenkins (b. 1952) has written a book about these quarrels titled *Jesus Wars*.[1] However, anyone who has studied the New Testament and the earliest Christian theologians knows that Christians have always considered Jesus Christ God incarnate and worshiped him alongside the Father and the Holy Spirit. During the second century, Greek philosopher Celsus wrote a book against Christians titled *On the True Doctrine* (178) in which he stated that Christians worshiped

---

1. Philip Jenkins, *Jesus Wars* (San Francisco: HarperOne, 2011).

a man as God. To Celsus this seemed stupid, but the point is that it demonstrates that second century Christians believed in and worshiped Jesus as God incarnate.

Nowhere in the New Testament is Jesus recorded as claiming to be God. However, as many orthodox New Testament scholars and theologians have demonstrated, Jesus made claims about himself that amounted to consciousness of being God. Jesus forgave sins as if he were the one sinned against. He accepted disciple Thomas's worship of him as "my lord and God." The apostle Paul wrote that Jesus was "in the form of God" (Philippians 2:6), and the first chapter of Colossians exalts Jesus Christ as creator of everything. Most of all, the Gospel of John opens with a ringing affirmation of Jesus Christ's identity as the "Word" who was in the beginning with God and was God.

In the classic book *Mere Christianity*, C. S. Lewis rightly argued that if Jesus was not God, he was a charlatan or a madman, because of his actions and words about himself. At his trial, Jesus was charged with making himself equal with God and did not deny it. Theologian Wolfhart Pannenberg (1928–2014), with whom I studied theology, validly argued for the historicity of Jesus' resurrection and argued that the resurrection means that God validated Jesus' claims of equality with God. God would not have raised a blasphemer from death.

Many heresies about the person of Jesus Christ arose in ancient Christianity, and all of them are still around in the twenty-first century.[2] Among them were teachings that denied the deity of Jesus Christ, and these were dealt with by bishops, theologians, and rulers. In 268 Bishop Paul of Samosata

---

2. See my book *Counterfeit Christianity: The Persistence of Errors in the Church* (Nashville: Abingdon, 2015).

(bishop of Antioch) was excommunicated by fellow bishops because he taught that Jesus Christ was adopted by God the Father as his special human son but was not preexistent or ontologically (having to do with being) divine. Later, church leader Arius of Alexandria denied the ontological deity of Jesus Christ and was excommunicated by the Council of Nicea in 325. His heresy, Arianism, was a bit different from Paul of Samosata's, but both denied the deity of Christ.

The equal humanity and deity of Jesus Christ, Son of God and God the Son, has been a cornerstone of orthodox Christianity in spite of occasional denials even among Christians. The World Council of Churches requires member denominations to affirm that "Jesus Christ is God and Savior." When someone denies the deity of Jesus Christ, explicitly or implicitly, he or she cuts the cord of continuity with biblical and historic-orthodox Christianity and steps outside of and away from Christianity. That person's religion is another one, not authentically Christian. That has been the consensus of Christians for more than two thousand years.

Toward the end of the eighteenth century and beginning of the nineteenth century, a group of British and American Christians denied the deity of Christ and the Trinity and labeled themselves Unitarians. They began organizing churches centered around those denials. One of their most influential American pastor-theologians was Theodore Parker (1810–60), who, according to Dorrien, preached that "true Christianity is not about the death or divinity of Christ, but about the death of sin and life of holy goodness in our hearts."[3] Even progressive

---

3. Gary J. Dorrien, *The Making of American Liberal Theology: Imagining Progressive Religion, 1805–1900* (Louisville: Westminster John Knox, 2001), 99.

orthodox pastor-theologians like Bushnell opposed this as not authentically Christian. Eventually, however, something very much like Unitarian Christology filtered into mainline American Protestantism. Liberal theologians began to sound like Parker when they talked about Jesus. Boston University philosopher-theologian Borden Parker Bowne elevated Jesus Christ to the status of the model human being, the perfect human revealer of God, but that demoted Jesus Christ to the status of a man different from the rest of us in degree, not kind.[4] University of Chicago Divinity School theologian George Burman Foster (1858–1918) taught that "while it is improper to say that 'Jesus is God,' it is not improper to speak of Jesus as the supreme and saving revelation of God."[5] Also, according to Foster, "God is like Jesus—this is the gospel."[6] Like many later liberal Christians, Foster even taught the divinity of the human spirit.[7] That is either completely to redefine divinity or else to deify humanity! Many liberal Christians have followed Foster in this confusing and even heretical pattern of thought—a kind of Christianized religious humanism.

A contemporary of Foster's was Baptist theologian William Newton Clarke (1841–1912), who taught at Baptist Colgate Seminary and wrote the first American liberal systematic theology. According to Clarke and his protégé Harry Emerson Fosdick, "The divinity of Jesus consisted in his unique spiritual consciousness."[8] Fosdick, pastor of Riverside

---

4. Dorrien discusses Bowne's liberal Christology in ibid., 391.

5. Gary J. Dorrien, *The Making of American Liberal Theology: Idealism, Realism, and Modernity, 1900–1950* (Louisville: Westminster John Knox, 2003), 158.

6. Ibid.

7. Ibid., 158–59.

8. Ibid., 359.

Church in New York City, graced the cover of *Time* magazine twice. He was the primary popularizer of liberal Christianity in America during the first half of the twentieth century. For him, "To say that Jesus is divine is to affirm that God should be symbolized 'by the best personal life we know.'"[9] He spoke for most if not all liberal Christians when he said, "They call me a heretic. . . . Well, I am a heretic if conventional orthodoxy is the standard. I should be ashamed to live in this century and not be a heretic."[10] Historian of liberal Christianity Kenneth Cauthen says that for most liberal Christians, Christ "represents, not the incarnation of the second person of the Trinity, but the perfection of human personality. His divinity is his perfect humanity."[11]

Liberal pastor-theologian Washington Gladden preached that "the name which represents most fully the modern way of thinking about Jesus Christ is that of Albrecht Ritschl."[12] Ritschl was second only to Schleiermacher in German theology during the nineteenth century. Many American liberal Protestant students flocked to Germany to hear him teach. They brought back his version of liberal Christianity and taught it in American mainline Protestant seminaries. Ritschl taught that when Christians affirm the divinity of Jesus Christ, they mean that Jesus Christ has the value of God for them. Jesus was the inaugurator of the kingdom of God, which is God's highest good. Because Jesus' life was unequaled in

9. Ibid., 381.
10. Ibid., 379.
11. Kenneth Cauthen, *The Impact of American Religious Liberalism*, 2nd ed. (1962; Lanham, MD: Univ. Press of America, 1983), 211.
12. Washington Gladden, *Present Day Theology* (Columbus, OH: McClelland, 1913), 129.

devotion to the kingdom of God, he has the value of God. God realized his highest good in the man Jesus and his way of life. Ritschl denied the preexistence of Jesus Christ except in God's mind. God always foresaw and anticipated the appearing of the man Jesus and the kingdom of God in him.[13]

According to Gladden, one of the primary Ritschlians of American theology, Jesus Christ is "the ideal of humanity realized."[14] In true liberal fashion, Gladden argued that Christians need to "overcome" the idea of a "great gulf" fixed between God and humanity: "Divinity is finite in man; humanity is infinite in God."[15] Jesus' divinity, then, was his perfect manhood or humanity. Gladden spoke clearly about his liberal view of Jesus Christ when he wrote, "When we speak of the Incarnation we mean that in the life of Jesus of Nazareth, simple, human, brotherly as we have learned to see it, God is revealing to all who have eyes to see what he himself is like, and what we would fain have all men become."[16] Again, the issue orthodox Christians have with this "degree Christology" (similar in structure to Paul of Samosata's adoptionism) is not what it affirms but what it denies about Jesus. Yes, Jesus was the perfect revelation of God and of humanity as God wants us to be, but that is not the "all" of the incarnation. If it is, then there can be no reason why other humans cannot be divine! This view of the incarnation has two major defects. First, it denies the incarnation (which means God become

---

13. For a fuller exposition of Ritschl's theology, including his Christology, see chapter 2.b in my *The Journey of Modern Theology: From Reconstruction to Deconstruction* (Downers Grove, IL: InterVarsity Press, 2013).

14. Gladden, *Present Day Theology*, 130.

15. Ibid., 137.

16. Ibid., 145.

flesh). Second, it opens the door to the pluralism of saviors—something many liberal Christians eventually affirmed—that there can be other saviors besides Jesus Christ.

Henry Churchill King's liberal colors showed most brightly when he titled his chapter on Christology "Christ as the Supreme Person of History."[17] According to King, Jesus Christ was "the supreme revelation of God," but only the Father is actually God. Echoing Unitarians, he wrote that "the religious need of the strict unity of God is very great,"[18] and he emphasized the humanity of Jesus Christ at the expense of his ontological deity. For him, the deity of Christ meant "the practical lordship of Christ."[19] Jesus Christ is "the Ideal realized,"[20] with "the Ideal" referring to the realization of the "value and sacredness of the person."[21] King also wrote that "Christ must be human that he may be divine" and that "he is the supreme self-revelation of God."[22] All of these wonderful things said about Jesus Christ fall far short of orthodox Christianity, in which Jesus Christ is God incarnate, the second person of the Trinity taking on human nature, God the Son living a human life.

When surveying liberal Christian thoughts and sayings about Jesus Christ and God, one has to wonder whether liberal Christian pastors and theologians were attempting to keep what they considered educated, sophisticated American Christians from wandering away into agnosticism

---

17. Henry Churchill King, *Reconstruction in Theology* (New York: Macmillan, 1901), 185.
18. Ibid., 193.
19. Ibid., 194.
20. Ibid., 245.
21. Ibid., 235.
22. Ibid., 243.

or Unitarianism. What other reason could they have to deny the ontological deity of Jesus Christ? Nothing scientific conflicts with classical, orthodox Christology. Nor is orthodox Christology illogical or irrational. It may be a mystery, but that does not count against it unless one is allergic to mysteries, which would then seem to cause one to run from quantum physics and many other areas in modern science. Whatever their motive was and is, liberal Christian thinkers cut the cord of continuity between their thoughts and teachings and biblical-historical, orthodox Christianity in Christology more than anywhere else.

Throughout this book, I have treated L. Harold DeWolf as a primary case of a moderately liberal Christian theologian. He wanted to distance himself from the pack of increasingly radical liberal thinkers and wrote that "the author of the present volume [*The Case for Theology in Liberal Perspective*] is not 'liberal' in any meaning of the term as is now commonly understood in American theological circles."[23] That was his self-assessment in 1959, when some liberal theologians like German-American Paul Tillich were questioning God's existence. There were rumors of a "Christian atheism" and "death of God theology." Those movements became public in the 1960s and created tremendous controversy—even among liberal Christians. However, DeWolf echoed the thinking of Gladden, Clarke, and other liberal theologians about Jesus Christ. His Christology was decidedly low because it was merely functional. For him, Jesus Christ functioned as God but was not ontologically divine; Jesus revealed God to

---

23. L. Harold DeWolf, *The Case for Theology in Liberal Perspective* (Philadelphia: Westminster, 1959), 11.

humanity. Here is DeWolf's typically liberal estimation of Jesus Christ: "The life and death of Jesus constitute a high revelation of what man may be, by the help of God."[24] Once again, it must be pointed out that a conservative, orthodox Christian does not necessarily disagree with such an estimation of Jesus Christ. Jesus Christ was human and the image of God was perfect in him; his life and death did reveal what a human person would be if he or she were perfect spiritually. But unless more is said about Jesus Christ—that he was also the incarnation of God—the door is left wide open for there to be other saviors, other perfect humans. In true liberal fashion, DeWolf left the strong impression that he believed that Jesus Christ was different from the best of humanity only in degree and not in kind.

According to liberal theologian Delwin Brown, Christians today need a "naturalistic Christology," which means one that does not depend on anything supernatural such as the preexistence and descent of the Son of God into Mary, becoming the God-man Jesus Christ.[25] So, according to Brown, with many liberal Christians in agreement, "Jesus is the re-presentation of a divine grace that is mediated in varying ways in all times and places."[26] This is an ideal expression of what I have here called "degree Christology." Jesus is different from other humans only in degree, not in kind—a godly man, but not God.[27] However, Brown saw the danger and attempted to head it off by saying that Jesus is more than a mere model or

24. Ibid., 78.
25. Clark H. Pinnock and Delwin Brown, *Theological Crossfire: An Evangelical/ Liberal Dialogue* (Grand Rapids: Zondervan, 1990), 158.
26. Ibid., 162.
27. Ibid., 168.

example to imitate.[28] However, the "more" is difficult to see when he says that "empirically considered, it is hard to argue that the grace of Christ is absolutely the best."[29] Immediately after that, he advocates pluralism—the idea that there are other saviors besides Jesus Christ. "I do not attribute to Jesus some sort of metaphysical singularity."[30] Beneath this low Christology lies Brown's belief that God is universally but not uniformly incarnate in all things.[31] If this were only an expression of the orthodox belief in God's omnipresence, that would be fine, but it is surely more than that. It is an affirmation of a universal presence of God in all things in the same way, even if to a lower degree, as in Jesus Christ. As Brown said, for him Jesus Christ is simply the "re-presentation" of God's universal incarnation in all reality. Whether this elevates all reality to divine status or lowers Jesus Christ to mundane status is unclear. To me the latter seems most likely.

A question an orthodox Christian might want to ask Brown and other liberal Christians is this: Is Jesus Christ worthy of worship? Ought anyone to worship him? If the answer is no, the cutting of the cord of continuity with biblical-orthodox Christianity is definite. Christians have always worshiped Jesus Christ. Jesus Christ accepted the disciple Thomas's worship. If the answer is yes, then, given that his incarnation is different only in degree and not in kind from God's incarnation in everything, why not worship everything? Where does one cross a line from worshiping trees—wrong—to worshiping Jesus—right?

---

28. Ibid., 162–63.
29. Ibid., 165.
30. Ibid., 168.
31. Ibid.

Liberal theologian Donald E. Miller reduces Jesus Christ to a "symbolic form" subject to change in every generation.[32] Although he does not offer a detailed Christology in *The Case for Liberal Christianity*, Miller apparently believes that Jesus is the symbol that mediates Christians' experience of "the Reality" that "stands both within and beyond our humanly created symbols."[33] The task of the liberal church, he says, is to reinterpret "the symbolic form of Jesus"[34] so that it offers "human wholeness . . . confidence in the ultimate meaningfulness of human existence."[35] Apparently, what matters about Jesus Christ is the symbol, not the historical or transcendent reality. He comes close to saying that taking Jesus Christ as more than a symbol is idolatrous: "To reify is to engage in idolatry."[36] (*Reify* means to interpret a symbol literally as actual—historically, for example.)

Miller is an example of how slippery liberal Christians can be. He writes, "I presently feel comfortable reciting the [Nicene] creed without editing it or feeling a pang of conscience if I affirm something that I do not literally believe."[37] One is tempted to gasp at this admission. Where is the honesty in verbally and even orally affirming that Jesus Christ is "truly God and truly man" and at the same time thinking, "But, of course, I don't believe that"? I'm sure that Miller would respond that he does believe it symbolically, but not literally. But I wonder what he would think of someone

32. Donald E. Miller, *The Case for Liberal Christianity* (San Francisco: Harper and Row, 1981), 20.
33. Ibid.
34. Ibid., 137.
35. Ibid., 37.
36. Ibid., 18.
37. Ibid., 5.

who said to his fiancée during the wedding ceremony that he would love her "till death do us part," while thinking, "But I mean that only symbolically, not literally." The creed is meant to be recited only by those who believe it. A cynic might object, "What does *literally* mean when we are talking about something as unique as the incarnation?" The simple answer is that *literally* means "really and not only symbolically."

Liberal theologian Peter Hodgson uses philosopher Hegel to express his Christology. For Hodgson, as for Hegel, the incarnation of God in Jesus Christ means "the actualized unity of divine and human nature."[38] According to Hegel as interpreted by Hodgson, God as absolute Spirit is actualizing himself (or itself) in and through humanity's spiritual and intellectual development toward unity, the ultimate synthesis of apparent opposites. The metaphysical unity of God and creation, God and human history and culture, is always "there" but always evolving. In Jesus Christ, Hegel claimed, God's self-actualization reached a climax before the end of history (prolepsis). Hodgson seems to agree with Hegel that "God actualizes godself in and through the world."[39] This is a version of panentheism. Hodgson denies, though, that Jesus Christ had or has a "literal divine nature."[40] Hodgson expresses perfectly the degree or functional Christology of nearly all liberal Christian thinkers: "Having a literal divine nature is not what makes Jesus to be the Christ but rather his function as revealer of divinity and mediator

---

38. Peter Crafts Hodgson, *Liberal Theology: A Radical Vision* (Minneapolis: Fortress, 2007), 50.
39. Ibid., 45.
40. Ibid., 51.

of reconciliation; he is one filled by the power of the Spirit to manifest love and endure anguish."[41] In a kind of throwaway line, Hodgson even states that there is an "element of truth" in Arianism—the ancient heresy that Jesus Christ was not God but God's greatest creature.[42] Arianism was considered the arch-heresy by orthodox, trinitarian Christians in the fourth century, and it was condemned by the councils of both Nicea and Constantinople. All orthodox Christians have rejected it as false and incompatible with authentic Christianity. If a person finds an element of truth in it, he or she should not worship Jesus Christ. That would be idolatry. Hopefully Hodgson does not worship Jesus Christ.

Finally, like Brown and many other liberal Christians, Hodgson affirms "a plurality of ways to God, of which Christ is one—for Christians, *the* way, but we can no longer claim the *only* way."[43] This is a major problem for any Christian attracted to liberal Christianity. It leads to pluralism, which might sound good but actually means a demotion of Jesus Christ to one savior among many and not really *the* Savior of humankind. This is a different religion from biblical, historical, orthodox Christianity. With pluralism of this kind, a line has been crossed into unchristian territory, and the cord of continuity with authentic Christianity has been cut. When someone who believes these things about Jesus Christ calls himself or herself Christian, it means nothing except he or she wishes to identify as such. But it would be like a communist calling himself a capitalist or a capitalist calling herself

---

41. Ibid.
42. Ibid., 34.
43. Ibid., 57, italics in the original.

a communist. Confusing and possibly self-deceiving is the best that can be said of such a claim. Some might dare to call it dishonest.

Inevitably someone reading this will assume I am suggesting that liberal Christians are unsaved and bound for hell. Not at all. That is not what I am suggesting. Only God knows whether a person is saved; that is surely what Jesus meant by commanding his followers not to judge people. God is the only judge when it comes to people's status in relation to him and their eternal destiny in heaven or hell. However, it is ridiculous to believe that no one should ever make any judgments about belief systems and truth claims. And sometimes it is necessary for Christians, however sadly and reluctantly, to say whether they think a group of people or individuals who claim to be Christian really count as Christian. If anyone thinks that is never called for, I can always find some example of a church or organization or individual whom *they* would say is not authentically Christian.

Contemporary culture highly values tolerance. Even many orthodox Christians think it is inappropriate to judge a church, an organization, or an individual who claims to be Christian as not authentically Christian. However, these Christians usually agree if the church or individual demonstrates hate. But the same Christians wince at judging someone who claims to be Christian as not Christian based on beliefs. All I can say is that if someone claims to be Christian but does not acknowledge Jesus Christ as God incarnate, he or she means something by *Christian* other than what it has always meant.

Beliefs matter. Christianity has cognitive content; it is not just a matter of ethical behavior. Many liberals believe that

Christianity is primarily about ethics, and ironically, many orthodox Christians seem to agree. A paradigm shift in the meaning of *Christian* has been occurring over the past two centuries and accelerating even among orthodox Christians. They may believe in Jesus Christ as God incarnate, but they destroy the meaning of their Christian confession if they allow it to include the denial of Jesus Christ as God incarnate.

Everyone who knew liberal theologian Marcus Borg agrees that he was one of the nicest men you could ever meet. Although I never met him, I have read his books, watched him speak online, and communicated with him by email. He was extremely gracious in responding to my questions and even my criticisms of his theology. However, sadly, I must say that his claim to be Christian cracked under the weight of his low Christology. Jesus was, he wrote in *The God We Never Knew*, a "Spirit person" but not divine.[44] Jesus was "the decisive revelation and disclosure of God," but not the only manifestation of God.[45] He was "a teacher of unconventional wisdom."[46] He subverted "monarchial ideas of God" and of human societies.[47] Did he rise from the dead? According to Borg, "Easter need not involve the claim that God supernaturally intervened to raise the corpse of Jesus from the tomb."[48] Borg, like all liberal Christians, denied the "creedal Jesus," the Jesus who was and is truly God and truly human.[49]

Borg's is another example of degree Christology, which sees

---

44. Marcus J. Borg, *The God We Never Knew: Beyond Dogmatic Religion to a More Authentic Contemporary Faith* (New York: HarperCollins, 1997), 91.

45. Ibid., 84.

46. Ibid., 99.

47. Ibid., 101.

48. Ibid., 93.

49. Ibid., 97.

Jesus Christ as different from the rest of humanity in degree, not in kind. According to orthodox Christianity, he was and is both. However true degree Christology may be (I don't think it is so at all), it is not true Christianity. It is Unitarianism in disguise. Heretics can be the nicest people. I might prefer some heretics or atheists over some orthodox Christians as my neighbors. However, Christianity is not a matter of niceness; it is a matter both of being a true follower of Jesus Christ and believing in him and in the fundamental doctrines of historic, orthodox Christian faith—whatever denomination.

John Shelby Spong influenced millions of people toward liberal Christianity through his numerous books, appearances on television talk shows, and lectures, both in person and online. In *Why Christianity Must Change or Die*, the retired Episcopal bishop and liberal theologian says that confessing Jesus Christ as "God's 'only son' [is] an arrogant claim."[50] Following that, he confesses that he favors "reopening the debate between Arius and Athanasius on the nature of Christ."[51] That is an astounding confession coming from even a retired Christian bishop! Athanasius (d. 373) was the long-suffering bishop of Alexandria, Egypt, throughout the Arian controversy over the deity of Jesus Christ and the Trinity. Athanasius wrote one of ancient Christianity's greatest classics, *On the Incarnation of the Word*, in which he strongly defended the equal deity of the Father and the Son of God, who became incarnate in Jesus Christ. This controversy was one of the worst in Christian history, and the outcome, that Jesus

---

50. John Shelby Spong, *Why Christianity Must Change or Die: A Bishop Speaks to Believers in Exile* (San Francisco: HarperSanFrancisco, 1998), 11.
51. Ibid., 19.

Christ is *homoousios* (of the same substance) with the Father, was one of its greatest victories. Apparently, if Spong had his way, Christianity would undo all that Athanasius and other ancient church fathers suffered for.

Spong boldly claims that Jesus' preexistence as the Word, the Logos, the Son of God, was not believed by anyone until the late first century.[52] How he knows this is unclear. One has to wonder about chapter 2 of the apostle Paul's mid-first-century epistle to the Philippians, where he confesses that Jesus "took on the form of a servant" even though he was "in the form of God." Spong denies the truth of much of the New Testament and of church tradition. "These sacred concepts," he writes, "involve us in a view of human life that is no longer operative."[53] "The vast majority of traditional Christian language has become inoperable. Jesus, as the agent of God's divine rescue operation, is not a Jesus who will appeal to or communicate with the citizens of this century."[54] In that particular context, he may have been referring more to the work of Jesus than his person, but his basic sentiment is the same with both.

Spong admitted about the first Christians that "in this Jesus, they had met God."[55] However, he continues by "demythologizing" everything supernatural about their experience of God and about Jesus Christ.[56] That includes the resurrection; it did not literally happen.[57] For Spong, as for most liberal Christians, what is important about Jesus Christ is "the Jesus experience"[58]

52. Ibid., 80.
53. Ibid., 84.
54. Ibid., 98.
55. Ibid., 110.
56. Ibid., 108.
57. Ibid., 116.
58. Ibid., 117.

in which the love of God is especially revealed in and through Jesus' humanity. Jesus, Spong affirms, "revealed that he somehow possessed the infinite depths of the life of God,"[59] and in him, somehow, "humanity and divinity flow together."[60] However, according to Spong, "Jesus did not differ from you and me in kind. . . . He differed only in degree, the degree to which the God-consciousness came to fullness in him."[61]

Unlike some liberal theologians, Spong at least acknowledges the possibility that he is simply creating a new religion.[62] At least his critics have "valid concerns" about that.[63] Perhaps, he mused, "we have entered the death throes of that venerable religious system we once called Christianity."[64] Overall, however, he does not believe that. Spong believes that Christianity can survive if it follows his lead—as he follows the lead of so many liberal theologians before him, back to Schleiermacher. Interestingly, though, it is liberal churches that are struggling to survive; conservative churches (including "renewalist" ones such as Pentecostal-charismatic) are thriving around the world.

One has to wonder which beliefs remain in Spong's rescue operation of Christianity for modern people. Certainly not Jesus Christ as God and Savior—the very cornerstone of biblical, historical, orthodox Christianity. Our conclusion must be that Spong's musing about critics' "valid concerns" is valid: he has created a new religion or created his own version

---

59. Ibid., 126.
60. Ibid., 131.
61. Ibid.
62. Ibid., 119.
63. Ibid.
64. Ibid.

of a new religion called Unitarianism that dates back to the early nineteenth century in America.

Finally, for this chapter, we come to Douglas Ottati, probably the most profound of all liberal theologians since Schleiermacher. His *A Theology for the Twenty-First Century* is a masterpiece of liberal Christianity. The only problem is that the title should probably be *A New Religion for the Twenty-First Century*. Even that, however, would be wrong since what he presents is largely an updated version of Schleiermacher's liberal Christianity. To be sure, Ottati *intends* to be reforming traditional Christianity and not inventing or reinventing a religion. Let the reader decide.

Like Spong, Ottati muses that German liberal theologian Ernst Troeltsch (1865–1923) may have been right when he predicted that Christianity might "morph" into something else; at least there is no guarantee that it won't.[65] In context, it seems that Ottati does not think his own theology represents the fulfillment of that prophecy. He does, however, think it possible that his own *Reformed* Christianity might morph into something historically disconnected from Reformed Christianity. He wants to avoid that break. But might his own theology be exactly what Troeltsch predicted: a new religion arising out of Christianity but no longer continuous with historical Christianity? Ottati thinks not, but if that can happen with Reformed theology, why not with Christianity in general, and why not his? His Christology can be seen as so different from orthodox Christianity that it represents a different religion.

The first hint of Ottati's departure appears when he

---

65. Douglas F. Ottati, *A Theology for the Twenty-First Century* (Grand Rapids: Eerdmans, 2020), 702–3.

describes what Scripture presents as "the event of Jesus Christ, *the paradigmatic-suggestion* in the light of whom we envision God as Creator-Judge-Redeemer."[66] Jesus Christ is "the paradigmatic suggestion"? What can that mean? Does this re-present the same trope of Christ as symbol we have seen before in liberal Christologies? Ottati bores deeper when he states that his Christology is based on "rich mythopoeic material" found in Scripture and Christian tradition.[67] The biblical picture of Christ is based not on factual records of historical events but on symbolic images with transforming power. Who is Jesus Christ for Ottati? He is "a person who discloses the fundamental divine dynamic and excellence at work in all creation."[68] Also, "He is the Logos of God made manifest in the life and ministry of a man from Nazareth."[69] Finally, "He is the paradigmatic disclosure of God's living wisdom, will, and purpose as well as of human life in appropriate relation to God."[70]

The orthodox Christian can say amen to all these wonderful things said about Jesus Christ, but he or she will think them insufficient to express the unsurpassable nature of Christ not only as the perfect human revelation of God but also as God himself among us as one of us. It is not enough to confess that Jesus Christ is "a God-shaped man"[71] or the appearance of "a new and ideal spiritual life."[72] These represent another liberal functional Christology that opens the door to the possibility of other saviors equal with Jesus Christ.

66. Ibid., 128, italics added.
67. Ibid., 357.
68. Ibid., 360.
69. Ibid., 361.
70. Ibid.
71. Ibid., 389.
72. Ibid., 388.

Once again, we see in Ottati an example of a serious departure from what has always been the heart of Christianity—Jesus Christ as unique and unsurpassable God and Savior. A word can be redefined only so thoroughly before it loses meaning. A religion can be revised only so thoroughly before it becomes something else.

Again, I am not suggesting that Ottati does not have a reconciled relationship with God. Nor am I suggesting that Ottati is intentionally dishonest or disingenuous; without doubt he does think of himself as a Christian, and many others consider him such. He is, as I suggested earlier, the best and most profound representative of that religious and theological tradition established by Schleiermacher (and he acknowledges parallels between his and Schleiermacher's theologies).[73] The question is whether Schleiermacher's tradition—the liberal Protestant tradition—is authentically Christian or a new religion entirely.

"Christianity is Christ" is an old saying among conservative, orthodox Christians. Many liberal Christians agree, but the question is, "*Who* is Christ?" Orthodox Christians and liberal Christians disagree about that. For orthodox Christians, Christ is God the Son, the second person of the Trinity, who became human through the event called the incarnation. He is God as well as paradigmatic man. He embodies the perfection of the image and likeness of God in humanity, something broken in all other human beings because of sin. But he does more than that; he also embodies God in human form. He is both God and man. The doctrine is called the hypostatic union—the union of two complete natures in one person—and it was

---

73. Ibid.

decided at the Council of Chalcedon in 451. Ottati at least pays lip service to Chalcedon's "basic accomplishment," but he ultimately rejects it as "a fractured dogma" using "speculative language."[74] For him, as for all liberal theologians who bother to address it, Chalcedon's definition (the hypostatic union doctrine) is at best a "semisymbolic statement" that points to "the paradigmatic character of the event of Jesus Christ."[75] Left unclear, not only in Ottati's Christology but in all liberal theology, is exactly what constitutes the event of Jesus Christ beyond a powerfully transforming symbol. For authentic Christianity and for orthodox Christians, the "event" of Jesus Christ is a living person who is God-for-us in human flesh, with whom we can have a personal, saving relationship, and through whom we come to know God because he *is* God.

74. Ibid., 392.
75. Ibid.

CHAPTER 6

LIBERAL THEOLOGY
AND SALVATION

At the heart of biblical, historical Christianity is the gospel—the good news that the human condition can be healed, made whole, and that God has begun that healing work and will finish it for those who rely on him. Concepts like sin, fall, grace, atonement, reconciliation, faith, and regeneration are central to the biblical story and have always held prominent positions in Christian thought and language. Orthodox Christian traditions emphasize and sometimes even define these concepts differently, but none deny that the human condition is so broken that only God can heal it and that God has reached out and begun to heal it in Jesus Christ. All orthodox Christian traditions have also always believed and preached that this healing of the broken human condition is supernatural—only God can do it, and he does it "from beyond," from outside the broken human condition. For orthodox Christianity, salvation is more than turning over a new leaf or spirit triumphing over nature. Salvation includes the Holy Spirit's triumphing over broken human nature, but it begins and happens from outside the broken human nature, even if God does end up transforming human nature from within.

Christianity is a religion of salvation, not self-realization. And according to the biblical and traditional gospel message, true salvation is by grace alone, as the apostle Paul declared in Ephesians 2:8–9. It is sheer gift that begins with the love of God and centers around the life, death, and resurrection of Jesus Christ. It enters humanity through that divine-human life, death, and resurrection received by faith and through trust in God, and continues its transforming work as broken but trusting individuals allow God's Holy Spirit to make them whole.

All that is to say that for biblical-orthodox Christianity in all its denominational varieties, salvation is God's supernatural work through Jesus Christ and the Holy Spirit even if, as some Christian traditions believe, the human person being saved must cooperate with that work. Jesus' death on the cross broke the power of Satan and sin, paid the penalty humanity owed to God because of sin, and reconciled God to humanity and humanity to God. Reconciliation is actualized when the sinner accepts it by faith. Jesus' resurrection conquered death for those who enter into communion with him by faith, and God sent the Holy Spirit to dwell within them, to heal their inward brokenness and make them holy, whole, once again in the image of God.

Again, admittedly, different orthodox Christians will emphasize different aspects of God's saving work through Jesus Christ and the Holy Spirit in different ways. But all have always agreed that this is something only God can do for and in us and that the change has already begun with Jesus Christ's life, death, and resurrection and the Holy Spirit's indwelling presence.

Underlying all of this is the common Christian belief that humans are, indeed, badly broken by sin, by defection from God, by inward corruption that mars the image of God. Also underlying it all is the belief that we are guilty before God and deserve punishment. Sin is an irreducible concept; it cannot be explained away as ignorance or not-yet-ness of spiritual evolution or formation. It is a fall from essence into existence, away from our intended true humanity in fellowship with God toward hellish existence in absolute estrangement from God. According to orthodox Christianity, our human condition is helpless apart from God's intervention to pull us out of it. But thanks be to God, he has intervened supernaturally in Jesus Christ, the Mediator, and the Holy Spirit, the Transformer.

All of this is found in the New Testament, the ancient church fathers, the medieval theologians, the Reformers, the post-Reformation pietists and revivalists, and all modern orthodox theologians and churches. It is the gospel, the good news that trumps the bad news. It is harshly realistic about our fallen condition and full of hope in God for overcoming it because of what God has done. Without this message, this belief in the gospel, Christianity is not Christianity.

In ancient Christianity a heretic named Pelagius (late fourth and early fifth centuries) preached a different "gospel" of self-salvation through good works. His alternative gospel came to be known as Pelagianism, belief that human beings can exercise their free will, doing works pleasing to God, and never need God's supernatural, intervening, reconciling, and healing grace. Some form of Pelagianism has haunted Christianity like a dark shadow down through the centuries, raising its ugly head repeatedly. It was condemned by the Council of Ephesus in 431 and again at the Council (Synod) of Orange in 529. All the Protestant Reformers harshly rejected it among the so-called Radical Reformers. Pelagianism has always existed in popular folk Christianity where people have wanted some credit for their own salvation. Clichés like "God helps those who help themselves" echo it. Most cults and heretical sects of Christianity preach some version of it. During the so-called Enlightenment at the beginning of modernity, many pseudosophisticated Christians embraced some form of it. That included the deists and Unitarians. Liberal Christians like Schleiermacher and Ritschl struggled with it, trying to avoid it, but ultimately failed because of their bias against anything supernatural. They also despised the "bloody" doctrine of the atoning death of Christ, considering it primitive, even disgusting. They developed alternative explanations of the cross event, reducing it to a martyrdom in which God displayed his love for humanity and entered into solidarity with humanity's suffering.

At the roots of all of liberal Christianity's defections from this gospel lie (1) a denial of the extreme brokenness of the human condition, (2) an optimistic hopefulness about humanity's ability to transcend nature, (3) a bias against anything supernatural such as divine interventions, (4) disdain for bloody sacrifices, including Jesus' atoning death on the cross, and (5) belief that everyone is already saved in the sense of reconciled with God even if they are not yet aware of it or living in communion with God (universalism). Liberal Christians shrink away from any talk of God's wrath, judgment (of people), and hell. They redefine *sin* and tend to view salvation as the human spirit cooperating with the divine Spirit, the two working together toward the conquest of the "drag" of nature that hinders the kingdom of God. Salvation, then, is an experience of fulfillment, liberation, harmony, and peace.

The foregoing is a rough sketch of liberal Christianity's alternative gospel, different from the one brought by Jesus Christ and preached by the apostles. This new gospel is fundamentally humanistic, relegating to the past—on the trash heap of primitive Christian thinking—everything about sin as rebellion, defection, guilt, condemnation, and salvation as God's unilateral intervention through blood sacrifice (the cross), bodily resurrection (conquering death), and the supernatural, transforming power of the Holy Spirit.

Friedrich Schleiermacher introduced this new and different gospel among mainline Protestant Christians in the first half of the nineteenth century. It had already been adopted by the Unitarians, but Schleiermacher brought it into mainline Christianity. To his credit, Schleiermacher tried to give it a non-Pelagian bent by emphasizing the necessity of the work of Jesus Christ and the church and its sacraments. Still, like the Unitarians, Schleiermacher preached and taught that all are already saved in the sense of reconciled with God. For him, as for the Unitarians, salvation is the realization of reconciliation with God and actual communion with God. For him, sin is the lack of God-consciousness, and salvation is the healing of God-consciousness through the mediation of the perfectly God-conscious man, Jesus Christ. His death on the cross was not a sacrifice for sins, a payment of a debt or penalty owed to God, but the "Redeemer's" identification with human suffering. Everything about the Christian gospel was redefined in Schleiermacher's theology. No doubt many of Germany's elites stayed in the mainline Protestant churches because of Schleiermacher's "rescue operation," rescuing Christianity from being despised as primitive, unbelievable for enlightened people. Otherwise, they may have found their way into deism or Unitarianism or just left the churches altogether. Schleiermacher showed them how it is possible to be thoroughly modern, enlightened, and at the same time Christian, but only at the expense of orthodox Christianity. He invented a new religion without admitting it.[1]

Gary Dorrien rightly begins his study *The Making of American Liberal Theology* with Unitarianism. Strangely, perhaps, Unitarianism lies in the background of liberal Christianity even though many early American liberal theologians abhorred it. Eventually liberal Christians succumbed to Unitarianism without knowing or admitting it. Unitarianism's essential Pelagianism appeared in its idea of the purpose of religion, which is, according to Dorrien, "to cultivate individual moral power."[2] Leading American Unitarian pastor-theologian Theodore Parker preached, "True Christianity is not about the death or divinity of Christ, but about the death of sin and life of holy goodness in our hearts."[3] Liberal Christian thinkers worried that Unitarianism discarded too much of traditional Christianity. "It threatened to extinguish Christianity" even

---

1. For a detailed exposition of Schleiermacher's theology, including his doctrine of salvation, see chapter 2.a in my *The Journey of Modern Theology: From Reconstruction to Deconstruction* (Downers Grove, IL: InterVarsity Press, 2013), 130–46.

2. Gary J. Dorrien, *The Making of American Liberal Theology: Imagining Progressive Religion, 1805–1900* (Louisville: Westminster John Knox, 2001), 56.

3. Ibid., 99.

as it "presented unprecedented opportunities."[4] Unitarianism opened the door to modern free thinking in religion, freeing religion from the shackles of tradition. Liberal Christian pastor-theologians looked for a third way between orthodoxy and Unitarianism and found it in Schleiermacher and other European liberal theologians' revised Christianity devoid of anything supernatural.

These early American liberal pastor-theologians drew heavily on another German theologian, Albrecht Ritschl, to state the positive aspects of their modernized Christianity. Ritschl and his followers in Germany built on Schleiermacher's "theology from below," nonsupernatural Christianity, but added the dimension of the kingdom of God as social reality dawning through political and economic reforms. Dorrien captures the spirit of early American liberal Christianity perfectly when he calls it "the liberal Victorian gospel": "The good news of the gospel is the triumph of the spirit over nature as mediated by the example and teaching of Jesus. Under the influence of Jesus, the perfectly God-conscious redeemer, human beings are liberated from the selfish impulses of their animal nature and transformed into persons in right relation with God. To be saved is to experience the fulfillment of one's moral and spiritual personality through the triumph of the indwelling Spirit of Christ over nature."[5] Of course, American liberal theology went through stages and permutations in relation to history, politics, and culture, but the essential idea of salvation remained ever the same. Traditional Christianity, the liberals believed, has both a husk and a kernel. The task of

4. Ibid., 110.
5. Ibid., 402.

modern theology is to separate the two, or at least to identify the difference between them. What is important is the kernel within the husk. The husk turns out to be whatever conflicts with modern, naturalistic sensibilities; the kernel turns out to be only what is acceptable to modern, naturalistic sensibilities and is still recognizably spiritual and even Christian.

Essentially, for all liberal Christians, the kernel is the transforming power of the example of Jesus Christ as the fully God-conscious man lovingly devoted to others, while the husk is the complex of miracle stories, myths, and dogmas that modern people find offensive. Put another way, the kernel is the inner triumph of spirit over nature, following the example of Jesus, and the husk is belief in divine interventions past or present that conflict with the alleged scientific worldview of the uniformity of nature.

Historian of American liberal Christianity Kenneth Cauthen agrees with Dorrien's view of the essence of the liberal gospel: "The liberal gospel is that the victory of spirit over nature may be won if men will appropriate the light and life which are mediated to them through the impact of the historical Jesus."[6] Eventually, for some liberal Christians, the "historical Jesus" became more of a symbol or an image than someone we can know much about. Still and nevertheless, salvation is always for liberal Christians imitating Christ's depicted way of life, loving God and loving what God loves, even if we cannot be certain of anything about Jesus' biography.

Historian William Hutchison reports that for liberal

---

6. Kenneth Cauthen, *The Impact of American Religious Liberalism*, 2nd ed. (1962; Lanham, MD: Univ. Press of America, 1983), 211.

Christians the human person is not radically sinful but free.[7] Freedom, not sinfulness, is humanity's "key attribute."[8] What then is sin? For the liberal theologians, man is "a potential co-worker with God, one whose terrible sinning was a way of retarding God's unfolding purpose."[9] Sin, then, is humanity's resistance to God's will, but it is not inherent in humanity. Humanity can choose either to be a coworker with God, helping build God's kingdom on earth, society organized by love, or to sink into selfishness. Salvation, then, is choosing to become a coworker with God.

Pastor-theologian Washington Gladden confessed that the "new theology"—liberal Christianity—does not believe in original, inherited sin.[10] Rather, it views sin as selfishness, egoism.[11] It is "a scornful and even contemptuous unbelief in God; it is the revelation of a consciousness which is essentially antisocial."[12] According to Gladden it can manifest as "rampant and riotous selfishness in human hearts."[13] But it is freely chosen; there is no necessity or inevitability in it. Unfortunately, most people do choose it to some degree. For Gladden, sin has consequences: "The penalty of sin . . . consists in the natural consequences of sin,"[14] which include "alienation from God and enmity against God." The root of sin lies in "the animal

---

7. William R. Hutchison, *The Modernist Impulse in American Protestantism* (New York and Oxford: Oxford Univ. Press, 1976), 247.

8. Ibid.

9. Ibid., 247.

10. Washington Gladden, *Present Day Theology* (Columbus, OH: McClelland, 1913), 73.

11. Ibid., 75.

12. Ibid., 76.

13. Ibid., 77.

14. Ibid., 79.

propensities in people."[15] Like most if not all liberals, Gladden did not believe in a historical fall of humanity.

So what is salvation? Gladden preached that salvation is "a new principle of life implanted in the heart,"[16] and that principle is selflessness and a social feeling toward others. This comes through repentance and belief, by which Gladden seemed to mean something like turning over a new leaf—away from self and toward the way of Jesus Christ.[17] "Salvation is through Jesus Christ. He shows us the way of life; by his great self-sacrifice he wins our confidence, and we become partakers of his spirit; through Him we come to know the true God and eternal life."[18] The result is heaven—"Harmony with God."[19]

How does the cross fit into Gladden's liberal theology? Gladden rejected substitutionary views of the atonement in favor of atonement as moral example and influence. "It is impossible . . . for any man of sane morality to admit the justice of punishing an innocent person for a guilty person's sins."[20] Atonement, Christ's reconciling work through his life and death, was "the revelation of God to men."[21] Also, "Atonement . . . is the name for the grief and pain inflicted by sin upon the paternal heart of God."[22]

As is so often the case with liberal theologians, the problems lie not so much in what Gladden affirms as in what he denies or neglects. Yes, sin is selfishness, but it is more. Sin is

---

15. Ibid., 80.
16. Ibid., 83.
17. Ibid., 83, 84.
18. Ibid., 87.
19. Ibid., 98.
20. Ibid., 155.
21. Ibid., 165.
22. Ibid., 169.

defection from God through rebellious disobedience to God's revealed will. Yes, sin is freely chosen, but it is also a condition into which human beings are born. We are born in sin, but we become guilty, alienated from God, when we freely act out the condition of sin through disobedience to God, something all people do insofar as they live to the age of accountability. Yes, atonement is a revelation of God's love and a moral influence toward self-sacrifice for others, but it is more. It is also God's act of reconciliation through Christ's death on the cross. Yes, salvation is turning over a new leaf, but it is God who turns it over through grace alone.

Sadly, Gladden's "new theology" is a different gospel than the gospel of the New Testament and traditional Christianity. Lacking is any profound sense of our sinful helplessness to be reconciled to God on our own. Lacking is any profound sense of God's justice and wrath. Lacking is any real call to repentance, sorrow for sin, and trust in Jesus Christ alone for salvation. Lacking is any real hell that awaits sinners who refuse God's offer of salvation through Jesus Christ. Gladden's gospel has the language of the New Testament and traditional Christianity, but he redefines words and concepts so that what actually appears is a thin humanism with Jesus Christ as example for moral living.

Henry Churchill King had little to say about sin and salvation in *Reconstruction in Theology*; what he believed about these important concepts must be discerned from what he says about other matters. For him, as for other liberal theologians, modernity requires that "the very definition of religion is changed."[23]

---

23. Henry Churchill King, *Reconstruction in Theology* (New York: Macmillan, 1901), 181.

Nothing stays the same. Doctrines must be practical rather than metaphysical. They are not about things-in-themselves but about daily Christian living and social transformation. The doctrine of sin must be relational; sin is turning away from the practical lordship of Jesus Christ, which means living "a deepening friendship with God."[24] Salvation means recognizing the "value and sacredness of [every] person"[25] because of the universal fatherhood of God.[26] Salvation also means the "quickening of the social conscience"[27] toward the kingdom of God as the real brotherhood of human persons.[28]

King was strongly influenced by Ritschl, whose whole lifelong project in theology was the "moralizing of dogma," throwing out doctrines and dogmas whose ethical fruitfulness could not be discovered and turning every doctrine and dogma retained toward social transformation, with the earthly, human, historical kingdom of God (a society organized by love) as the ideal. King's interest in salvation was not so much forgiveness or reconciliation with God as character formation—the shaping of a life of love following Christ's example.[29] Again, what comes across through King's account of sin and salvation, thin as it is, is something like turning over a new leaf. Salvation turns humans away from focus on self and toward focus on others, especially toward the kingdom of love shown in Jesus Christ's teaching and life.

It is ironic that King warned against the very thing he did:

---

24. Ibid., 200.
25. Ibid., 235.
26. Ibid., 171.
27. Ibid., 178.
28. Ibid., 238.
29. Ibid., 199–206.

"It is easy here to make one's protest against the old creeds so strong as seriously to weaken the hold of all Christian truth."[30] King protested against traditional doctrinal statements, systems, and doctrinal formulations, especially Calvinism. In the process, though, he let go of most Christian truth. In the words of the old saying, he threw the baby out with the bathwater—something typical of liberal Christianity.

Ethicizing theology is good; moralizing dogma is valuable. Some have done it without throwing the baby out with the bathwater. An example from King's own time is British evangelical pastor-theologian Peter Taylor Forsyth (1848–1921). In books like *Positive Preaching and Modern Mind*, the congregational minister advocated and practiced the "moralizing of dogma" without discarding traditional Christian doctrines such as original sin and salvation by the atoning death of Jesus Christ.[31] For example, he emphasized the humanity of Christ as the model for Christian ethical living but without denying the deity of Christ. He also reformulated the doctrine of the atonement to emphasize its moral influence without denying its objective achievement of reconciling God to humanity and humanity to God. Forsyth was progressive without being liberal theologically. He is a model for many progressive evangelicals.

The problem with liberal theologians and liberal Christians is that they go too far in reconstructing Christianity and theology. Evangelical theologian Millard Erickson (b. 1932) distinguishes between translating the gospel and

---

30. Ibid., 4.
31. Peter Taylor Forsyth, *Positive Preaching and Modern Mind* (London: Hodder and Stoughton, 1907).

transforming it.[32] Forsyth translated it for the modern mind; Gladden, King, and liberal theologians tend to transform it— into something other than authentic Christianity. Into what? I might not be too far off the mark to say they transformed the good news into the false gospel of early Unitarianism.

A century after Unitarianism arose in America, mainly in New England among Congregationalists, Gladden and King simply repeated Unitarianism's essence, with a Christian veneer. Early Unitarians did not neglect Jesus Christ or God, sin or salvation. They reinterpreted those doctrines, mainly in reaction against the harsh, rigid, and dogmatic Calvinism of their tradition. Gladden and King should have just admitted that they were essentially Unitarians who used the language of traditional Christianity but meant more or less what the Unitarians meant. That they didn't have to, that they could write and preach what they did within a mainline Protestant denomination (the American Congregational Churches), speaks volumes about what was going on in mainline Protestantism during their lifetimes and ministries. The same is happening today in American Protestantism.

Some historians of liberal Christianity distinguish between evangelical liberals and modernist liberals. Gary Dorrien dislikes that distinction while admitting there's some truth in it. According to him, however, all true liberal Christians are modernists.[33] However, even he recognizes some liberal theologians as being closer to evangelical reli-

---

32. Millard Erickson, *Christian Theology*, 3 vols. (Grand Rapids: Baker, 1983–85), 1:112–20.

33. Gary J. Dorrien, *The Making of American Liberal Theology: Idealism, Realism, and Modernity, 1900–1950* (Louisville: Westminster John Knox, 2003), 16.

gion than others. L. Harold DeWolf is one such case. DeWolf believed in and taught original sin as universal sinfulness; he denied only inherited guilt (the Augustinian doctrine that every child is born guilty of Adam's sin)—something many traditional Protestants have denied.[34] He wrote that humanity's true, essential nature is good, but "to be good is exceedingly difficult, while to be evil, one has only to let his impulses have sway."[35] He does not explain why. With regard to salvation, DeWolf wrote that the human person cannot be truly himself or herself "without the effort of a will transformed and turned beyond himself by the grace of God."[36] No doubt he was referring there to prevenient grace, typically a Methodist doctrine of God's aiding grace. Thus, DeWolf was not reducing salvation to merely turning over a new leaf, but he did seem to have in mind a kind of Christian moralism combining grace and effort.

Like many liberal theologians, DeWolf believed in universal salvation.[37] At the same time, however, he also called for both individual and social conversion—to the way of Jesus Christ. That way is following the "ethical requirements of Jesus . . . as far as individual, personal patterns of life are concerned."[38] DeWolf could be frustratingly vague at times, sounding both liberal and conservative. With conservative, orthodox Christian theology he affirmed universal sinfulness and need of salvation; with liberal, modernist Christian

34. L. Harold DeWolf, *The Case for Theology in Liberal Perspective* (Philadelphia: Westminster, 1959), 115–23.
35. Ibid., 123.
36. Ibid.
37. Ibid., 175.
38. Ibid., 146.

theology he believed that, in the end, all people will be saved even without conversion. His emphasis fell on the Christian life, and he implied that it could be lived simply by turning over a new leaf, making the right choices, and following the pattern of life exemplified by Jesus. Yet he also affirmed "Man as Divinely Confronted"[39] and called by God to repent and believe. Lacking was orthodox Christianity's strong emphasis on the supernatural grace of God for salvation, grace that gives the sinner the ability to repent and believe.

DeWolf clearly wanted to be evangelical in some sense; he did not regard himself as a thoroughgoing modernist. And yet he repeatedly called for Christianity to accommodate to modern culture. He was something of a prophet regarding his liberal colleagues and friends: "If we do not believe the Christian faith to be true in its basic assumptions, then we are not believers and it is only a mockery to call ourselves Christians."[40] The question is whether DeWolf himself deserved to be called a Christian in light of his Christology and weak soteriology (doctrine of salvation).

Liberal theologian Delwin Brown expressed a doctrine of sin without inherited corruption or guilt. "Sin," he wrote, "is the manifold way that we deny or distort ourselves as a part of spirit or as a part of nature. Sin is a denial of ourselves as God created us—as spirit-and-nature, as nature-and-spirit."[41] Brown did not follow the typical nineteenth-century liberal idea of salvation as spirit transcending or even conquering

---

39. Ibid., 115.
40. Ibid., 188.
41. Clark H. Pinnock and Delwin Brown, *Theological Crossfire: An Evangelical/Liberal Dialogue* (Grand Rapids: Zondervan, 1990), 103.

nature. He acknowledged the goodness of nature. His emphasis about sin was "social sin"—the many ways in which human beings live against the "divine lure" toward harmony. For him, as for many late twentieth-century liberal Christians, salvation was interpreted as something that happens *in* our history, especially liberation from oppression.[42] Brown's theological liberalism reveals itself most clearly in his assertion that grace is a "power in nature, in persons, in society, in economy, in history."[43] This is the immanence of God in soteriological terms; God is embedded graciously in all of reality. There seems to be no need of supernatural incursions or special actions; it is a matter of discovering and using the grace that is always already there.

In typical liberal-theology fashion, Brown denied the existence of a literal heaven and hell. For him, heaven and hell are the "permanence of every fulfillment and of every destruction" in this life and in history.[44] "The imagery of 'eternal life' connotes . . . the conviction that our lives, even now, have an ultimacy, an abiding meaning in an everlasting God."[45] For Brown, as a process theologian, God absorbs into himself everything that happens. God's life is either enriched or impoverished by what we do. Everything affects God and therefore affects the future as God is able or unable to influence the world toward good. Brown avoided answering the question of personal, subjective life after death. It is possible to read him as not believing in the afterlife, although he did

---

42. Ibid., 183.
43. Ibid.
44. Ibid., 239.
45. Ibid., 240.

not explicitly deny it. In that sense he seemed to break away from the consensus of liberal Christian theology about universal salvation.

Liberal theologian Donald Miller expressed salvation as "one's experience" of "the Reality" mediated by "the forms" (symbols) of Christianity.[46] Of all the liberal theologians surveyed here, Miller's thought is the most abstract. That's because of his wholehearted embrace of symbolic realism. For Miller, religion is about symbols, not history or miracles or supernatural revelations. The symbols may be revealed, but they arise "from below," from the experiences people have with "the Reality" (God). Miller's theology may be abstract; it is also subjective. He suggests little that's objective to hold on to, such as the historical resurrection of Jesus Christ. Certain religious symbols transform people in positive ways; that's what religion is all about. Salvation is the experience of being transformed positively by experiences of "the Reality" (God) through symbols, "the forms" of religion (including Christianity).

Liberal theologian Peter Hodgson turned to liberation theology to reconstruct a Christian doctrine of salvation. For him liberal theology *is* liberation theology, but on more levels than Latin American liberation theology.[47] According to Hodgson, "A diversity of independent ways of salvation appears in the history of the world."[48] There is no one way of salvation, but for contemporary American Christians, it is best

---

46. Donald E. Miller, *The Case for Liberal Christianity* (San Francisco: Harper and Row, 1981), 31.

47. Peter Crafts Hodgson, *Liberal Theology: A Radical Vision* (Minneapolis: Fortress, 2007), 69.

48. Ibid., 90.

to understand salvation as "liberated freedom."[49] Here is what he means by that: "An enhancement of life and diversity, a harmonious dwelling together of the whole cosmos, a struggle to heal tragic conflicts, a growth in love and freedom, enlightenment and wisdom, goodness and beauty."[50] So salvation for Hodgson, as for many liberal Christians, does not include forgiveness by God or reconciliation with God in any traditional sense; it is about social transformation. To be sure, it involves the individual, but the individual's salvation depends on the transformation of the whole cosmos. Exactly what God has to do with it all Hodgson leaves unclear. Also unclear is whether people need to repent and trust in God through Jesus Christ to be saved. It seems doubtful.

Again, the problem with Hodgson's account of salvation is not so much what it affirms as what it leaves out. An orthodox Christian can affirm that ultimate salvation includes cosmic transformation (Romans 8) and, together with the church fathers and the Reformers, will insist that salvation includes individual transformation by God's grace through faith (and some will want to add "works of love"). That individual transformation includes reconciliation with God, which requires repentance. Wholly missing from Hodgson's account of salvation, as well as most liberal accounts, is any idea of conversion—that the individual needs to be born again by God's Spirit through repentance and faith.

Liberal theologian Marcus Borg admits that "estrangement" from God and others and oneself is part of the human condition. For him, salvation is overcoming estrangement

49. Ibid.
50. Ibid., 91.

through "opening to God."[51] For him, salvation is multifaceted, but at its heart is "being reconnected to God."[52] Ultimately, this reconnection with God is a gift of God's grace; the only task for the human person is faith, which involves faithfulness, trust, and belief.[53] So far, so good. However, for Borg this being saved is a lifelong process; there is no conversion except that "we decide to take the first step"[54] in having a restored relationship with God. This is an expression of what is known in historical theology as semi-Pelagianism, the heresy that the initiative in salvation belongs to the human person. Whether Borg would agree, if pushed to explain himself, is questionable. However, overall and in general, Borg's account of salvation does not include any threat of hell if one does not receive the gift of God. For him, salvation is primarily this-worldly, having to do with life here and now, before death. He was agnostic about life after death and wrote, "At the center of the biblical understanding of salvation is a relationship with God in the present, whose gifts are freedom, joy, peace, and love and whose fruits are compassion and justice."[55]

Without doubt, of all the liberal theologians surveyed here, Borg stands out as one of the most orthodox, and yet there is still so much of biblical-orthodox Christianity missing in his theology. His doctrine of salvation lacks the biblical emphasis on radical discontinuity between the old life and the new, the experience of what the Bible calls regeneration, being "born from above" (John 3:3). Typical of liberal Christianity

51. Ibid., 111, 114.
52. Ibid., 160.
53. Ibid., 169–71.
54. Ibid., 170.
55. Ibid., 175.

is an emphasis on continuity and a neglect of radical divine intervention to create something new. Also missing is the biblical call to repentance and the very real threat of hell for not repenting.

John Shelby Spong is perhaps the most aggressive of all liberal Christian theologians when it comes to rejecting traditional, orthodox, and especially conservative Christian views of salvation. With regard to the traditional Christian view of Christ's atonement, he wrote that "I would choose to loathe rather than to worship a deity who required the sacrifice of his son."[56] For him, Jesus' death on the cross was a profoundly tragic martyrdom of a great prophet, not a saving sacrifice for sins. Spong rejected all traditional Christian beliefs about sin as "guilt-manipulation" and upheld a positive view of humanity. For him, original sin is simply the truth that "all human beings are still caught in the struggle to become our deepest and truest selves."[57] Predictably, Spong is a universalist in terms of individual salvation; there is no hell. He laid his liberal cards out on the table quite clearly when he wrote, "I . . . must leave behind most of the baggage of heaven and hell, all of the theistic understandings of God, and . . . those legendary and fanciful attempts to interpret Jesus as the incarnation of a theistic external deity."[58] Yet after all that, he held out hope for "some sense of eternity."[59]

Liberal theologian Douglas Ottati writes about salvation under the rubric of "Human Life" in *A Theology for the*

---

56. John Shelby Spong, *Why Christianity Must Change or Die: A Bishop Speaks to Believers in Exile* (San Francisco: HarperSanFrancisco, 1998), 95.

57. Ibid., 97.

58. Ibid., 219.

59. Ibid.

Twenty-First Century. There, in true liberal fashion, he proposes that salvation simply means what Paul Tillich taught: "It is as though a voice were saying: 'You are accepted . . . by that which is greater than you.'" Ottati continues in his own words: "Accept the fact that God *is* the God of grace and that God will be God. In that acceptance there is assurance, as well as the courage to participate in situations replete with promises and risks."[60] Although Ottati frequently mentions and quotes Swiss theologian Emil Brunner (1889–1966), he neglects Brunner's emphasis on salvation as both gift and task. For Ottati, so it seems, salvation is solely gift without task. He does discuss sanctification, growth in grace, even good works, but not as having anything to do with divine acceptance. He takes Luther's *simul justus et peccator* (righteous and sinner at the same time) to an ultimate extreme and leaves us with the notion that all people are accepted by God regardless of their act or decision of faith, their trust in Jesus Christ or lack of it. The result, seemingly, is a psychologized doctrine of salvation that is intended to make people relax from fear of God into a kind of Stoic acceptance that they are accepted without any requirement of stepping outside of themselves into the realm of God's grace by faith that repents of sin, turning away from sin and self toward God and being inwardly transformed, given a new heart supernaturally by the Spirit of God, who comes to dwell within them. Ottati's doctrine of salvation, for all its rigor about political commitments for those who accept that they are accepted, ends up being therapeutic. All can be assured that they are automatically saved by grace.

---

60. Ibid., italics in the original.

What, then, is salvation in liberal Christianity? It depends on which liberal Christian you ask, but the consensus among liberal theologians is that salvation is a process of becoming our better selves together with God, who is somehow enhanced by that process. Still, most liberal theologians want to say something about human sin and God's grace, but sin gets reinterpreted as falling short of our true, better selves, and grace gets reinterpreted as God's helping presence in our struggle to become better. Going back to the father of liberal Christianity, Friedrich Schleiermacher, sin is lack of God-consciousness. Salvation is the increase in God-consciousness. Grace is God's help in increasing God-consciousness. Lacking in all liberal Christianity is any sense of human helplessness to do anything pleasing to God or to restore a right relationship with God. Lacking is any sense of real lostness, of utter alienation from God, of condemnation. Lacking is any sense of intervening, supernatural grace through Jesus Christ, especially his sacrificial death that reconciles God to us and us to God if we repent and believe. Lacking is any sense of a future real heaven and hell.

Again, as with other beliefs, liberal Christians have cut the cord of continuity between their doctrines and those of Christians before them, at least before Schleiermacher, the founder of this new kind of Christianity. Sure, there were free thinkers and heretics before Schleiermacher, but he was the first deeply embedded church theologian to cut the cord completely and construct a new religion with Christ at its center. "With Christ at its center" is misleading, however, because standing alongside Christ at the center was and is the human being. Christ does not stand alone at the center of liberal Christianity (if at all). Beginning with Schleiermacher, the focus of liberal Christianity's attention is the potentially good human being. In this view, everyone needs to surpass nature with spirit into full spiritual actualization by turning over a new leaf with God's help. A human-centered religion has then replaced real Christianity, Christianity as it has ever been before, New Testament Christianity, Christianity of the church fathers and mothers, Christianity of the Reformers, Christianity of the evangelical, Catholic, and Orthodox faiths, Christianity focused on God's gracious intervention to save the lost, to give hope to the hopeless, to forgive.

Liberal Christianity, if it is Christianity at all, is what the apostle Paul called a "different gospel." It is a false gospel, assuming the biblical-orthodox gospel is true. Those who embrace the gospel of liberal Christianity ought to admit that it is not authentically Christian. They may call it good news, but those who know how helpless we humans are to have a right relationship with God on our own, apart from God's supernatural, intervening grace and power, know that this liberal gospel is bad news because it cannot communicate what we do not already tell ourselves or want to know by ourselves. And what we tell ourselves or know by ourselves, about God, sin, and salvation, is usually in our own interests and does not cost us anything. It is, as a student called it, "weak sauce," and worse. It may be worse; it may be spiritual poison because it betrays the truth God has revealed about himself and us and how we can find fulfillment, hope, joy, and peace.

CHAPTER 7

THE FUTURE IN
LIBERAL THEOLOGY

Is there an orthodox Christian doctrine about the future?
Many conservative Christians confuse certain popular
beliefs about the future with "what the Bible teaches." Popular
books about the end times, biblical prophecy, the rapture,
and the Antichrist have caused this confusion. Most of these
popular Christian books express or fictionally illustrate certain opinions about what the Bible teaches about the future.
Some Christian denominations have actually elevated some of
these opinions to the status of required doctrines.

For example, premillennialism may or may not be true;
nonetheless, I think there are good biblical reasons for believing in it. Premillennialism is the belief that after Christ returns
to earth, he will rule and reign personally, bodily (in his glo-
rified body), on earth for a thousand years. Premillennialists
base this on Revelation 20, among other passages. They believe
that during this future millennial reign of Christ on earth,

Satan will be bound, kept from tempting people. Some of the earliest church fathers taught a version of premillennialism, but this interpretation of the Bible and the future was never elevated to the status of dogma, what all Christians must believe, until the early twentieth century, and even then only by some extremely conservative, fundamentalist Christians. The vast majority of Christians consider it at best a doctrine, not a dogma of orthodox Christianity.[1]

However, the Bible contains much prophecy about the coming of God's messiah at the end of human history as we know it. That Jesus Christ will return to earth has always been believed by orthodox Christians of all major traditions. The Apostles' Creed says that Jesus Christ will come again to judge the living and the dead. All Christians believed in Christ's return to earth to judge the nations and to open up heaven to those who embrace his love and grace—until the rise of liberal Christianity with Schleiermacher. From Schleiermacher on, liberal theologians have generally regarded talk of the parousia—the return of Christ and events surrounding it—as symbolic, metaphorical, not at all to be taken literally or as actual events in the future.

This constitutes another major liberal defection from biblical-orthodox Christianity. Some liberal Christians go so far as to suggest that the world will end in a vast sun explosion, and that will be the end of our world, with nothing to come after that. Humanity itself may cease to exist. Some

---

1. For more about premillennialism in traditional, orthodox Christianity, including among the church fathers, see *A Case for Historic Premillennialism: An Alternative to "Left Behind" Eschatology*, ed. Craig L. Blomberg and Sung Wook Chung (Grand Rapids: Baker Academic, 2009).

liberal Christians deny subjective immortality—belief in individual, conscious life after bodily death. Instead, they embrace objective immortality—belief that when a person dies, he or she will simply live on in God's memory. Other liberal theologians express agnosticism about the nature of life after death, but all deny (explicitly or implicitly) hell as everlasting punishment of the wicked.

Christian theology about the consummation of humankind and life after death is called eschatology, and this chapter is about liberal Christians' eschatological beliefs and teachings. It will demonstrate that liberal theologians who influence liberal Christians cut the cord of continuity between themselves and orthodox Christianity so thoroughly that they ought to stop calling themselves Christians.

There is little doubt that the father of liberal Christianity, Friedrich Schleiermacher, believed in life after death, but he was reticent when it came to describing it. In the words of twentieth-century theologian Reinhold Niebuhr, Schleiermacher probably thought that we should not want to know too much about the furniture of heaven or the temperature of hell. Whether Schleiermacher believed in a literal (real) hell is doubtful. He was a believer in universal salvation, as were all of his faithful liberal followers. What did he believe about the parousia? That it is a symbol of the coming of God-consciousness to individuals and to the human family. He did not believe in a literal return of the man Jesus Christ to judge the world and establish his kingdom forever.[2]

It is interesting that Gary Dorrien has little to say about

---

2. Friedrich Schleiermacher, *The Christian Faith*, ed. H. R Macintosh and J. S. Stewart (1830; Edinburgh: T&T Clark, 1948), 707–9.

eschatology in his three-volume history of American liberal theologians' beliefs. The reason probably is that liberal theologians themselves have said little about eschatology! Eschatology seems to have dropped away from liberal Christianity, except perhaps the "already" of the traditional "already but not yet" duality of Christian belief in the kingdom of God. In traditional Christian thought, the kingdom of God through Jesus Christ is already present, but in a hidden way; its fulfillment is right now *not yet*—that is, future. Christians have long disagreed about the details of eschatology, but they have always agreed that Jesus Christ will return to establish the fullness of his kingdom—whether on this earth within history or beyond it in a new heaven and new earth (or both, as in premillennialism). Liberal theologians have often spoken and written about the question of life after death, as I will show here. However, their ideas about life after death leave much to be desired. One liberal pastor preached at the funeral of my wife's grandfather Helmer. The pastor said, over the body in the casket, "Helmer is gone; we will never see Helmer again. But God holds Helmer in his memory." The pastor was a recent graduate of a well-known liberal seminary.

Washington Gladden, one of the first liberal American pastor-theologians, taught the reality of heaven and hell, but he identified them with conditions of spiritual consciousness in the present life, following Schleiermacher closely. "Heaven is harmony with God."[3] "Hell is alienation from and enmity with God."[4] "Heaven and hell are already begun in

---

3. Washington Gladden, *Present Day Theology* (Columbus, OH: McClelland, 1913), 98.

4. Ibid., 102.

us; in many of us they are contending for the mastery, and it seems not certain yet with all of us whether the angels or the demons will win."[5] Yet Gladden also believed in the immortality of the soul, though according to him immortality is conditional. "The tendency of sin is to the diminution of being. . . . I believe that persistent sin must finally result in the extinction of being."[6] This is an expression of what some call annihilationism, the belief that the wicked will finally be annihilated rather than tortured in a literal hell for eternity. On the same page where he affirmed hell as annihilation, Gladden strongly hinted at the possibility of universal salvation: "Evil may come to an end through the final restoration to virtue of all wandering and sinning souls."[7] Obviously, when he wrote *Present Day Theology*, he had not reached a conclusion about hell.

A few pages later, however, Gladden suggested that "heaven and hell are not, primarily, places, they are states of character."[8] Then, on the same page, he concluded that "probably" the next life will be a continuation of this one—in terms of character associations: "We shall find the associations and occupations that are congenial."[9] Without doubt, Gladden did believe in personal, subjective life after death. "The conscious life of the spirit does not terminate with the death of the body; that the physical organism is the shelter or the temple of an immortal life; that death is but the departure of the immaterial intelligence from its material habitation;

---

5. Ibid., 111.
6. Ibid., 113.
7. Ibid.
8. Ibid., 115.
9. Ibid.

that when the body returns to dust as it was, the spirit returns unto God who gave it."[10] He even argued for some kind of new body, a resurrection of sorts, while denying continuity between the present body and the new one.[11] The new one, he suggested, will be "ethereal" as opposed to physical.

Like many conservative and liberal Christians of his time, and before, Gladden seemed to embrace postmillennialism—belief that the fullness of God's kingdom through Jesus Christ may come through human endeavor: "Just as soon as the children of men can learn to believe that the way of love is the way of life heaven will be here."[12] However, he had little to nothing to say about the parousia, the second coming of Jesus Christ.

One interpretation of Gladden's theology is that there was within it, as within many early American liberal Protestants, a struggle between traditional, orthodox Christianity and the new theology stemming from Germany, from Schleiermacher and Ritschl. Gladden held on to as much of traditional Christianity as he could while embracing the new theology, the "present day theology." Missing almost entirely from his eschatology, however, was any teaching about the glorious return of Jesus Christ to earth or any of the events surrounding it, such as judgment and new heaven and new earth. His theology clearly focused almost exclusively on this-worldly concerns, even though he believed in a conscious existence of the individual after death. This was typical of Victorian-era liberal theology; eventually even conscious existence of

10. Ibid., 202.
11. Ibid., 215.
12. Ibid., 119.

the individual after death would become problematic for late twentieth-century liberal Christianity.

Liberal theologian Henry Churchill King, in *Reconstruction in Theology*, a classic of early American liberal Christian theology, said almost nothing about eschatology, a glaring omission. Toward the end of the book, he wrote about the kingdom of God in purely social terms: "The kingdom of God is within, indeed— the reign of God, who is love, in the individual heart."[13] "Love *is* the giving of self in personal relations. The Kingdom of God, therefore, is, necessarily social—not personal and social, but social because personal."[14] What to make of this omission of explicit reconstruction of eschatology? First, King was probably a postmillennialist like Gladden; he probably thought of the kingdom of God as a social order ruled by love within human history. But he probably was agnostic about the future otherwise. His silence about life after death and the return of Christ is deafening. Perhaps he spoke or even wrote about it elsewhere, but a book titled *Reconstruction in Theology* should at least hint at beliefs about such fundamental Christian doctrines. It seems reasonable to conclude that King, like many other early twentieth-century American liberal theologians, was almost exclusively concerned with this world, with history, with social salvation. Under the influence of philosopher Immanuel Kant, they tended to reject "speculation" about the "noumenal realm"—the realm of things beyond experience.

Unlike King, liberal theologian L. Harold DeWolf included an entire chapter on "The End of All Things" in his book *The*

---

13. Henry Churchill King, *Reconstruction in Theology* (New York: Macmillan, 1901), 238.

14. Ibid.

Case for Theology in Liberal Perspective. The Methodist theologian affirmed, "If in the end God's just love is to be vindicated, there must be, for individual persons and for the race, a life beyond death."[15] Like Gladden, he affirmed some kind of resurrected bodies while leaving the details vague.[16] DeWolf cautiously suggested a final restoration of all to communion with God without affirming universalism: "It would seem that punishment after death must be regarded as administered in the *hope* and with the *purpose* of stirring the sinner from his complacent pride and preparing him for the redeeming work of God's love."[17] Clearly DeWolf believed in subjective immortality while denying a Platonic natural immortality of the soul as if it were a spark of the divine.[18] However, he left us to wonder about the details, even about the possibility of universal salvation.

With regard to the parousia, DeWolf affirmed a "coming again of Christ,"[19] but "this need not be taken to mean a spectacular bodily descent of Jesus the Nazarene. The imagery used in the Gospels to describe the Parousia symbolizes mystery, and the divine majesty."[20] Having said that, which sounds like symbolic realism, he turned around and, on the same page, articulated "confidence that his coming will be in character, as he is known in Jesus of Nazareth." This is, to say the least, unhelpful. What people want to know, and what orthodox Christianity has always answered with yes, is whether the

---

15. L. Harold DeWolf, *The Case for Theology in Liberal Perspective* (Philadelphia: Westminster, 1959), 172.

16. Ibid., 174.

17. Ibid., 175, italics in the original.

18. Ibid., 172–73.

19. Ibid., 179.

20. Ibid.

incarnate Lord Jesus Christ will return to this world in the future. Apparently DeWolf was unsure how to answer that, which is a major signal of liberal thinking in theology. At least his silence is better than later liberal theologians' outright denying the return of Jesus Christ.

In typical moderate liberal fashion, DeWolf concluded his section on eschatology vaguely: "Just as surely as the whole human episode on earth will one day end ... all who have lived on earth will then be under the same Father's care and judgment and love in other realms beyond death."[21] While some Christians may be satisfied with such theological mush, the intelligent, thinking Christian wants to know more, and both the Bible and Christian tradition offer more: a new heaven and new earth where God will dwell with his people forever, and no more sin, sickness, or death.

Unfortunately, even most moderate liberal Christians, like DeWolf, cannot say this "more." Why? What is stopping them? One possible answer is a reaction to an overly detailed, literalistic interpretation of biblical teachings about the future. No doubt some Christians, like Dante regarding purgatory and hell, have gone too far, allowing their imaginations to run away with them. Will there be "mansions over the hilltop" prepared for the saved? Literal mansions? One popular gospel song says so. Perhaps DeWolf and other moderate liberal theologians wanted to shy away from that kind of popular folk Christianity. But why not correct it rather than neglect its concerns and questions? One example of a highly intelligent, educated, intellectual Christian theologian who does this is N. T. Wright in

21. Ibid., 180.

his magnificent book *Surprised by Hope: Rethinking Heaven, the Resurrection, and the Mission of the Church.*[22]

Some conservative Christians "know" too much about the future and about life after death, and most liberal Christians "know" too little. Gladden, King, and DeWolf knew, or at least said, too little. Orthodox Christianity knows a lot about the future. How to interpret the biblical language and imagery is not easy, but simply to sweep most of it away and replace it with mushy hope for some vague future life with God is unhelpful, especially to those facing death. They want to know more, and orthodox Christianity offers more. What more? At least the confidence of being with Christ after death and eventually being raised to newness of bodily life like Christ's own resurrected body (1 Corinthians 15). Orthodox Christians may disagree about details of the future, but they have a robust and well-grounded hope, a confidence that there will be fulfillment of life with Christ and proper fear that unrepentant sinners will face judgment and hell. For almost two thousand years, Christian pastors and theologians even spoke about the rewards in heaven for those who suffered for the truth and for Christ. The almost complete disappearance of reward talk may be evidence of the trickle-down effect of liberal theology's minimalizing of eschatology.

Like many liberal Christians, theologian Delwin Brown settled for vague hopes for the future of both the individual after death and for the world. In his dialogue with conservative theologian Clark Pinnock, Brown rejected literal interpretations of heaven and hell in preference of nonliteral

---

22. N. T. Wright, *Surprised by Hope: Rethinking Heaven, the Resurrection, and the Mission of the Church* (New York: HarperOne, 2009).

interpretations of both. For him, heaven and hell point to the "permanence of every fulfillment and of every destruction," even if not the permanent, conscious existence of every person after death. Without using the phrase, he came close to affirming objective immortality. "The imagery of 'eternal life' connotes . . . the conviction that our lives, even now, have an ultimacy, an abiding meaning in an everlasting God."[23] He avoided offering a clear, unequivocal answer to Pinnock's questions about conscious life after death. He treated the biblical language about eschatology as "a cluster of linguistic symbols."[24] About individuals' afterlife, Brown asserted, "People cannot 'go' to some 'place' called heaven or hell."[25] He attempted to qualify that by talking about an "interrelatedness" of persons taken "everlastingly in the reality of God."[26] Brown should not complain if someone like Pinnock finds this language hopelessly (pun intended!) vague and unhelpful.

In *Theological Crossfire*, his dialogue with Pinnock, Brown says little, if anything, about an ultimate victory of good over evil. Brown is a process theologian; any confident expectation of a future victory of God over evil is contrary to the basic ideas of process theology.[27] At least in this dialogue with Pinnock, Brown says nothing about a second coming of Christ, although he would likely consider that a powerful symbol of

23. Clark H. Pinnock and Delwin Brown, *Theological Crossfire: An Evangelical/Liberal Dialogue* (Grand Rapids: Zondervan, 1990), 240.
24. Ibid., 242.
25. Ibid., 246.
26. Ibid.
27. See *Process Philosophy and Christian Thought*, ed. Delwin Brown et al. (Indianapolis: Bobbs-Merrill, 1971). This edited volume includes a historical and analytical introduction to process theology by Brown. It also includes numerous essays by leading process theologians. All agree that God, being essentially limited in power, cannot guarantee a final, eschatological victory over evil.

the positive influence Jesus Christ has on individuals and on history—insofar as they freely choose to accept and live out Christ's mission for transformation.

Liberal Christian thinker Donald E. Miller, in *The Case for Liberal Christianity*, has virtually nothing to say about the future, either of the individual after death or of the world. He offers only one hint at what he hopes for: "What would religion be if it did not comfort, offer hope, and suggest that temporal existence is not all that meets the eye? Surely a religion that did not inspire confidence in the future and comfort in the present would be a unique species of religion."[28] However, he does not flesh out what that hope and confidence in the future means. One may be justified in thinking he believes all we have, as Christians reading the Bible and Christian tradition, are symbols. Exactly what they are or mean is never explained.

Liberal theologian Peter Hodgson dispenses entirely with literalistic hopes of an ultimate end to the struggle between good and evil. For him, God is a spirit of pure freedom providing all of creation with impulses toward unity and harmony, but whether those will ever be fully realized is uncertain. According to him, "God creates the world, becomes incarnate in Christ and other savior figures, and sends the Spirit toward an end—an end that can never be fully grasped but includes such goals as an enhancement of life and diversity, a harmonious dwelling together of the whole cosmos, a struggle to heal tragic conflicts, a growth in love and freedom, enlightenment

---

28. Donald E. Miller, *The Case for Liberal Christianity* (San Francisco: Harper and Row, 1981), 144.

and wisdom, goodness and beauty."[29] Given what else he says in *Liberal Theology: A Radical Vision*, it is doubtful that he intends "God creates the world, becomes incarnate in Christ . . . sends the Spirit" to be taken literally. These are symbols of the Hegelian dialectic which Hodgson critically embraces, in which God is incarnate in the whole cosmos and especially history, all the time, and is always struggling together with the world and humanity to establish harmony and beauty. Left completely out of this "radical vision" of Hodgon's liberal theology is any realistic hope for individual life after death and a return of Christ to establish his fulfilled kingdom.

Liberal New Testament scholar and theologian Marcus Borg confessed to being "agnostic" about "an afterlife."[30] "Nevertheless," he also confessed, "I think there is something rather than nothing."[31] Experiences such as near-death experiences, he says, at least call into question dogmatic reductionist worldviews that deny any life outside of the natural-biological.[32] However, the most Borg could say about life after death is that "we do not die into nothingness but we die into God."[33] He declined to be more specific about the afterlife. For most people, Christian and non-Christian, "dying into God" is too vague to be helpful or to give confident hope about the future. The Bible is so much richer in its teachings. Admittedly, much of what the Bible says about the afterlife is metaphorical, but even the metaphors tell us much more than that we "die into God." There is

29. Peter Crafts Hodgson, *Liberal Theology: A Radical Vision* (Minneapolis: Fortress, 2007), 90–91.
30. Marcus J. Borg, *The God We Never Knew: Beyond Dogmatic Religion to a More Authentic Contemporary Faith* (New York: HarperCollins, 1997), 171.
31. Ibid.
32. Ibid.
33. Ibid., 175.

the biblical and traditional Christian belief in resurrection bodies, fullness of life (eternal life) in a new heaven and new earth, liberated from bondage to decay, and free of sin, sickness, and death. Borg and other liberal theologians might be satisfied with a vague belief in dying into God, but the Bible offers more, as does Christian tradition. At least Borg believed in subjective immortality rather than objective immortality, in which life after death means only being held in God's memory or living on in one's impact on history.

Liberal retired Episcopal bishop John Shelby Spong stated that he *did* believe in life after death, but he adamantly insisted that it is not like popular or conservative religious pictures of it. According to him, "The content of this reality of life beyond the boundaries of death is so radically different from anything that has been proposed by the religious systems of the past that it is all but unrecognizable."[34] Throughout his chapter on "Eternal Life Apart from Heaven and Hell," Spong criticizes and deconstructs traditional beliefs about life after death and the future. All are mythical at worst, symbolic at best, and simply beyond belief for modern people. The clearest affirmation he offers is "some sense of eternity in which my being, differentiated and defined by the power of love, is joined with the being of others who are at one with the Ground of all Being."[35]

Liberal Christianity leaves us hopeless about our futures and the future of the world; biblical and orthodox Christianity offers us hope in Jesus Christ for everlasting, eternal life, together with him and all the saints, God's people, in heaven.

---

34. John Shelby Spong, *Why Christianity Must Change or Die: A Bishop Speaks to Believers in Exile* (San Francisco: HarperSanFrancisco, 1998), 201.

35. Ibid., 219.

Liberal Christianity leaves us unfulfilled when it comes to our sense of justice for the victims of extreme oppression, for even the perpetrators of the Holocaust will be "at one with the Ground of all Being," to use Spong's words. Liberal theology goes far beyond Niebuhr's warning about not wanting to know too much about the furniture of heaven or the temperature of hell; it throws out any meaningful heaven and hell and, at best, holds out hope of some featureless life beyond the grave. The return of Jesus Christ in glory, divine judgments, a fulfilled kingdom of God, a new heaven and a new earth free of sin, sickness, and death, where there will be no more tears, all get treated as myths or symbols. We are left almost entirely with this world and virtue as its own reward.

Now we turn to the most recent and perhaps most profound of liberal Protestant theologians since Schleiermacher, his contemporary disciple Douglas Ottati, liberal Christian theologian par excellence. Unlike some of his liberal cohort of theologians, he delves deeply into the biblical materials about eschatology and wrestles with many points of Christian tradition. He is not interested only in deconstructing "much conventional talk of 'life after death,'" even though, he admits, "there are serious spiritual and theological difficulties" with it.[36] After a detailed analysis of various eschatological proposals by many biblical scholars and theologians, past and present, Ottati finally offers his own position while noting that "we are dealing here with something that . . . seems shrouded in ambiguity and in mystery."[37]

36. Douglas F. Ottati, *A Theology for the Twenty-First Century* (Grand Rapids: Eerdmans, 2020), 709.

37. Ibid., 728.

His position, however, is not very different from those of other liberal theologians we have encountered. Its clearest expression arrives in a footnote where he favorably quotes another liberal theologian named Brian Gerrish: "For myself, I think the weight of tradition advises Christians, despite modern skepticism, not to surrender the belief in personal survival [of death] too quickly and yet to remain frankly agnostic about its nature."[38] Ottati affirms that God is the answer to the question of hope, but that all talk about resurrection, continuing spirits and selves, and worlds to come remains "opaque."[39]

Ultimately, Ottati comes across as more in touch with the Bible and Christian tradition, more attuned to the various theological proposals about eschatology, but in the final analysis he is no more helpful in establishing hope for the future than other liberal theologians. Whether he believes in personal, conscious, bodily existence in heaven, let alone hell, remains unclear. One can reasonably interpret some of what he says about life after death as affirming objective, but not subjective, immortality. And he has almost nothing to say about a return of Jesus Christ, a parousia, in or at the end of history.

Why are liberal Christian intellectuals and their disciples in the pulpits and pews so reticent about eschatology? What motivates their skepticism about the subject? One possible answer is overreaction to Christian speculation about the

---

38. Ibid., 734. The quotation is from B. A. Gerrish, *Christian Faith: Dogmatics in Outline* (Louisville: Westminster John Knox, 2015), 316. Gerrish is perhaps the foremost scholar of Schleiermacher and his theology, having written a book about the German father of modern liberal theology titled *A Prince of the Church: Schleiermacher and the Beginnings of Modern Theology* (Eugene, OR: Wipf and Stock, 2001). I heard the lectures that constitute this book at Rice University in about 1980. The book was originally published by Fortress Press in 1984.

39. Ibid., 734.

subject. So much nonsense has been written and preached about both heaven and hell that even thoughtful conservative believers finally shy away from the topic. However, there is nothing inherent in being educated, scholarly or intellectual, or even modern that requires such skepticism. Have they simply thrown the baby out with the bathwater? N. T. Wright is one modern, educated, intellectual Christian scholar who has shown, especially in *Surprised by Hope*, that eschatological expectation can be at least somewhat detailed.

Frankly, the majority of liberal Christian churches exist near secular or vaguely church-related colleges and universities. One might be justified in thinking that these liberal thinkers and those who follow them are under the mistaken impression that being modern and intellectual requires giving up belief in eschatological realities, with the one exception of some vague notion of life after death.

Insofar as they have given up belief in bodily resurrection and the return of Jesus Christ to establish his fulfilled kingdom and a new heaven and new earth, free of sin, sickness, and death, liberal theologians have departed from Christianity. Theirs is a secularized, gutted, emptied eschatology with no recognizable continuity with biblical, historical, orthodox Christian eschatology. Liberal eschatology leaves people hopeless in the face of death, evil, and the destruction of the environment. The future they describe looks bleak at best.

CHAPTER 8

THE CRISIS OF
LIBERAL THEOLOGY

Even liberal Christian theologians acknowledge that liberal Christianity is in crisis. For several decades, its followers have been dwindling. Liberal churches have seen their pews emptying, their membership rolls shrinking. Major liberal-leaning Protestant denominations have lost millions of members. Sociologist of religion Dean Hoge is one of many scholars who have studied this decline in so-called mainline Protestant churches. His explanation was published in the journal *First Things*: "In response to the currents of modernity, denominational leaders promoted ecumenism and dialogue, but they did not devise or promote compelling new versions of a distinctively Christian faith. They did not fashion or preach a vigorous apologetics."[1] Many sociologists of religion suggested

---

1. Dean R. Hoge, "Mainline Churches: The Real Reason for Decline," *First Things*, March 1993, https://www.firstthings.com/article/1993/03/mainline-churches-the -real-reason-for-decline.

that mainline, liberal-leaning denominations and churches became reflections of secular culture and lost their prophetic power; they accommodated to modern, secular culture so much that members lost interest. Where did this liberal accommodation to culture begin for the declining churches? The simple answer is in their seminaries. For more than a century, mainline, liberal-leaning Protestant seminaries in America have been promoting liberal Christianity. As Swiss theologian Karl Barth (1886–1968) famously found out during his first pastorate, liberal theology just doesn't preach.

Orthodox Christians of many denominations have long criticized liberal theology as heretical and even apostate. As mentioned earlier, Presbyterian theologian J. Gresham Machen launched a blistering attack on liberal theology in *Christianity and Liberalism*: "Despite the liberal use of traditional phraseology modern liberalism not only is a different religion from Christianity but belongs in a totally different class of religions."[2] Many people who did not read the book assumed Machen was talking about something other than real liberal Christianity, as described in his book and here. This misunderstanding caused great consternation; even people who would agree that real liberal Christianity is not authentically Christian, if they bothered to study it, object to such seemingly harsh judgments against anyone who identifies as a Christian. Of course, Machen was not judging anyone's salvation or even anyone's personal Christian faith; he was (and I am) judging a theology as not authentically Christian. However, as everyone

---

2. J. Gresham Machen, *Christianity and Liberalism* (Grand Rapids: Eerdmans, 1923), 7.

knows, it is difficult to separate the persons from their ideological commitments.

Before and after Machen's book, many books, articles, and pamphlets against liberal theology poured forth, mostly from fundamentalist authors and publishers. Some of those are embarrassing even to orthodox Christians. Some of them are shockingly ill-informed, relying solely on secondary literature, most often by other fundamentalists. Machen knew liberal theology firsthand; he studied it in Germany at the centers of liberal theology. A century later, I have made a thorough study of liberal Christianity and its theology firsthand. I have come to the same conclusion Machen did, and I think any orthodox Christian, however progressive they might be, must agree that liberal Christianity is not authentically Christian. Liberal Christianity is a religion that venerates Jesus but does not adhere to anything like orthodox Christianity, except in its phraseologies.

Liberal Christianity and its organizations have lost many members and are by no means as culturally relevant or dominant as they were in their heyday. According to Dorrien, "By 1895, [the liberal] movement dominated the discourse and institutions of the American Protestant establishment."[3] That dominance lasted for at least a century within the so-called mainline Protestant denominations and institutions. Liberal theology still dominates many denominations, even if in a somewhat altered form. Nevertheless, without doubt, liberal Christianity has faced several crises after 1895 and has had to adapt to survive. There's nothing inherently wrong with that;

---

3. Gary J. Dorrien, *The Making of American Liberal Theology: Imagining Progressive Religion, 1805–1900* (Louisville: Westminster John Knox, 2001), 262.

all religious movements adapt to survive. However, liberal Christianity never really adapted so as to restore continuity with biblical, historical, orthodox Christianity.

One crisis was brought about by the two world wars. Before World War I, liberal Christianity had been generally optimistic about humanity and history; humankind would climb upward toward the kingdom of God on earth by education, social reform, science, and enlightened religion. The two world wars forced liberal theology to become more realistic about humanity and history, acknowledging that they are infinitely perfectible and that the kingdom of God on earth, as a social order organized by love, is probably not expected. Chastened liberalism took the place of humanistic, overly optimistic liberalism, and some liberal theologians deserted the movement, adopting existential anxiety about humanity and history, and even rediscovering original sin as a universal brokenness within humanity, both individuals and the race itself. Reinhold Niebuhr was one such deserter from liberal theology, even though fundamentalists always considered him liberal.

A second crisis is less clearly tied to any cause; throughout the second half of the twentieth century and into the twenty-first century, liberal Christianity, as I have described it here, faced a loss of credibility and power. The pews of liberal churches largely emptied (with many exceptions, of course), and liberal-leaning denominations, denominations that allowed liberal theology to flourish in their seminaries, colleges, and universities, declined in numbers and influence.

Gary Dorrien is honest about this second crisis. Throughout his three-volume history of American liberal theology, he mentions it, but not despairingly. He is one liberal theologian who is attempting to breathe new life into liberal Christianity. Toward the end of the third volume, he argues for "an unnoticed renaissance" of American liberal theology, while admitting that "American liberal theology [was] locked in crisis since the 1930s and taken for dead even by its friends since the 1960s."[4] According to Dorrien, liberal theology in America is not just surviving but flourishing with new vitality. If he is right, I find that frightening. I fear he is right, as many disillusioned former fundamentalist students (and others) are slip-sliding away from mere progressivism into full-blown liberal theology. Today, progressive Christianity is often just a halfway house from which people emerge into full-blown liberal theology in one of its varieties. Marcus Borg, for example, is extremely attractive to many of them.

Here I want to mention some criticisms of liberal Christianity and its theology by some of its own spokespersons, beginning with Dorrien. Speaking of early twentieth-century liberal Christian leaders, he says, "Only belatedly did they question whether they had granted too much authority to modern culture in the course of liberating American Christianity from its scriptural and ecclesiastical houses of authority."[5] The same question could be put to Dorrien and every liberal Christian! Are they asking themselves this question *now*? Not seriously enough. Writing about liberal Methodist theologian DeWolf's immanent critique of the liberal Protestant churches of his

4. Gary J. Dorrien, *The Making of American Liberal Theology: Crisis, Irony, and Postmodernity, 1950–2005* (Louisville: Westminster John Knox, 2006), 513.

5. Dorrien, *Making of American Liberal Theology: Imagining Progressive Religion*, 411.

time, Dorrien bemoaned that "liberal congregations neglected the Bible, showed little or no interest in evangelism, and sneered at revival preaching. Their own preaching was sentimental and psychologized; they prized gradualism and niceness, looked for God only in the universal, and had no concept of divine judgment or the fear of God."[6]

Dorrien also quotes liberal theologian Van Harvey (1926–2021), who quipped that for liberal theology, "'Christianity' became merely a re-presentation of modern self-understanding."[7] According to Dorrien, "Theologian Stephen Webb puzzled that contemporary liberals found it possible to write so much despite believing so little."[8] Dorrien himself complained that "liberal theologians . . . often found themselves speaking a language that had little currency in congregations."[9]

My experience of being a member of two liberal Protestant churches, serving on the staff of one and on the executive committee of another, convinces me that all these criticisms are still valid. One church was a downtown Baptist congregation in a state capital. The materials used in Sunday school classes were antifundamentalist and prosecular, pro–liberal politics, pro–mental and emotional health. The preaching was most often good advice, but lacked the gospel. The pastor, a former Southern Baptist, deeply disillusioned with that denomination's conservative turn, told the congregation that the New Testament's talk about Satan and demons was merely

6. Dorrien, *Making of American Liberal Theology: Crisis, Irony, and Postmodernity*, 25.
7. Ibid., 516.
8. Ibid., 522.
9. Ibid., 529.

a primitive way of talking about mental and emotional diseases and dysfunctions. Under one-on-one cross-examination, he admitted to me that he did not think the Gospels are historical but contain symbolic and mythical representations of spiritual experiences. That congregation dwindled down to mostly empty pews during my four years there.

I served as minister to youth and director of Christian education at a mainline Presbyterian church for three years. There was little that was theological about the church; a few members seemed to have some interest in theology, and I attempted to teach them their own Presbyterian theology. The pastor, however, was a graduate of a liberal mainline Protestant seminary, and his sermons were mainly therapeutic. He was intent on assuring the mostly aged congregants that their lives were "of meaning and value to God." Notably missing from sermons, Bible studies, and adult Sunday school classes, except the ones I taught, was anything about Christian doctrine. The church had at one time been a thriving neighborhood congregation that drew in hundreds of people. At the time I was on staff, however, it was dwindling severely to a handful of mostly senior citizens. I noticed that the presbytery was closing down churches and merging them. During my three years, two Presbyterian congregations closed their doors and merged with our church, which didn't seem to increase its vitality.

At the same time (1970s and 1980s), conservative churches in America were booming. This caused sociologist of religion Dean Kelley to write *Why Conservative Churches Are Growing.*[10]

---

10. Dean M. Kelley, *Why Conservative Churches Are Growing: A Study in Sociology of Religion* (New York: Harper and Row, 1972, 1977).

His thesis and conclusion were that conservative churches of many kinds were offering a version of Christianity that was robust and vital, not a mere reflection of modern culture with a spiritual veneer on it. The book was an indictment of liberal Christianity by one of its own.

Church historian Kenneth Cauthen includes several pages of criticism of liberal theology in *The Impact of American Religious Liberalism* and argues that "the whole perspective of liberalism needs to be corrected in the light of a better model of reality than that which is appropriated too uncritically from modern culture."[11] He focuses especially on liberal theology's overemphasis on God's immanence to the neglect of God's transcendence and on its lack of realism about sin. Church historian William Hutchison agrees halfheartedly with Cauthen, criticizing "the acceptance of Christianity's cultural involvement" in liberal theology while nodding toward its positive potential if reconsidered.[12]

One of the early prototypes of American liberal theology I have used to represent classical liberal Christianity, Henry Churchill King, warned fellow liberals that "it is easy here to make one's protest against the old creeds so strong as seriously to weaken the hold of all Christian truth."[13] Unfortunately, King himself did just that. Another prototype, L. Harold DeWolf, warned that "liberal theology often accommodates to culture by too easily identifying the ethical requirements of

---

11. Kenneth Cauthen, *The Impact of American Religious Liberalism*, 2nd ed. (1962; Lanham, MD: Univ. Press of America, 1983), 223.

12. William R. Hutchison, *The Modernist Impulse in American Protestantism* (1976; New York and Oxford: Oxford Univ. Press, 1982), 311.

13. Henry Churchill King, *Reconstruction in Theology* (New York: Macmillan, 1901), 6.

Jesus with the moral customs of the day, especially as far as individual, personal patterns of life are concerned."[14]

Evangelical theologian Clark Pinnock, in his dialogue with Delwin Brown, cautions that the main problem with liberal theology is "its apparent willingness to break with the foundational proclamation. . . . It leaves the way open to reduce and distort the Word of God under the pressure of modern ideas."[15] This is what I have been arguing throughout this book, albeit using different language—liberal theology cuts the cord of continuity between itself and biblical, historical, orthodox Christianity.

Liberal theologian Donald Miller put his finger on "the danger in liberalism," which is "that the Christian message may become a mirror reflection of the spirit of the age."[16] A liberal Christian theologian who came to reject liberal theology for that very reason was Methodist Thomas Oden (1931–2016). Oden publicly declared his conversion to orthodox Christianity in *After Modernity . . . What? Agenda for Theology*.[17] Oden had been a liberal professor of theology and continued to serve as a professor of theology, but from an orthodox Christian perspective. He authored numerous books expounding orthodox and conservative, but nonfundamentalist, Christianity. He was embraced warmly by the American evangelical community of theologians (such as the Evangelical Theological Society). He

14. L. Harold DeWolf, *The Case for Theology in Liberal Perspective* (Philadelphia: Westminster, 1959), 146.

15. Clark H. Pinnock and Delwin Brown, *Theological Crossfire: An Evangelical/Liberal Dialogue* (Grand Rapids: Zondervan, 1990), 36.

16. Donald E. Miller, *The Case for Liberal Christianity* (San Francisco: Harper and Row, 1981), 34.

17. Thomas C. Oden, *After Modernity . . . What? Agenda for Theology* (Grand Rapids: Zondervan, 1992).

was a rare example of a true liberal Christian intellectual who turned away from liberal thought to orthodox Christianity without leaving Protestantism to join Eastern Orthodoxy or Roman Catholicism.

Oden's critique of liberal theology, of his own early theology, was that it was captive to the spirit of modernity, which is transient and contrary to the basic impulses of the Bible and Christian tradition. He also argued that it is inimical to the human soul, which naturally longs for and needs supernatural grace. In some ways, Oden was progressive after he converted to orthodox Christianity. He believed in the full equality of women in churches. He rejected literalistic readings of the early chapters of Genesis (e.g., young earth creationism) and of biblical apocalyptic literature (e.g., dispensationalism). He was most definitely not ever a convert to fundamentalism. People who think there are only two kinds of Protestant Christianity—fundamentalist and liberal—have never read Oden! And, of course, he is not alone. There are numerous moderate-to-progressive, evangelical Protestant scholars who are not fundamentalists but are biblically committed and orthodox with regard to Christian doctrines. Among them were and are John Stott (1921–2011), Donald G. Bloesch (1928–2010), N. T. Wright (b. 1948), Richard Bauckham (b. 1946), Stanley J. Grenz (1950–2005), Scot McKnight (b. 1953), and G. C. Berkouwer (1903–96), to name only a few.

My experience as a Christian theologian for forty years is that the majority of people attracted to liberal Christianity are Christians raised in rigidly fundamentalist homes and churches who have moved into progressive Christianity—whatever that means, exactly—and are not satisfied with that vague halfway house. As self-identified progressive Christians, which, in the third decade of the twenty-first century usually means pro-LGBTQ in every aspect and level of church life, they feel the pull of all-out liberal Christianity. Having departed from fundamentalism and skipped over moderate evangelical Christianity, they find progressive Christianity fuzzy, unclear, mediocre, and on a trajectory toward liberal Christianity. Most of them move in that direction. At some point they slip away and fall over the cliff from authentic Christianity into full-blown liberal Christianity. They may remain warmhearted toward God and still love Jesus; they may still read their Bibles devotionally; but they no longer believe in miracles, the incarnation of God in Christ, the bodily resurrection of Jesus, or a real hell awaiting those who reject God's grace and mercy. They shrug at the doctrine of the Trinity out of disinterest because, "after all, it's a mystery." They devote their whole attention as Christians to social justice causes. For them, the cognitive content of orthodox Christianity shrivels up and dies except as a collection of symbols, relics, artifacts—like heirlooms with little appeal or use but kept out of some vague sense of loyalty to the past.

Progressive Christianity is not a tradition or a movement or even a real identity. It is simply a label used by many different individuals who do not want to be thought of as conservative and who are attracted to social-justice issues, often to the neglect of evangelism, sound doctrine, and traditional Christian norms of belief and life.

Liberal Christianity, on the other hand, is a tradition that grew out of a movement that began with Friedrich Schleiermacher in Germany and was exported to America mostly by students of Albrecht Ritschl. Typically, it does not really explain anything except God-consciousness or theocentric piety or how to be a Christian without believing any of the traditional doctrines of the historical, biblical, orthodox churches. For all its words, it is frustratingly vague, shallow, limp, unhelpful in answering life's ultimate questions. It is dying out except in certain mainline Protestant colleges, universities, and seminaries. There is no real life in it, and many of the people in the pews of America's churches have realized that and left, either to join conservative churches or abandon church altogether because, frustratingly, there are too few churches that are moderate—in between fundamentalist and liberal.

The message of this book to self-identified progressive Christians is: Beware of liberal Christianity, because it is not real Christianity at all. Look for and find a church, a seminary, whatever, that truly takes the Bible and orthodox doctrine seriously but is not cultic in its ethos, like most fundamentalist churches, seminaries, and other ultraconservative Christian organizations. Fundamentalism, described as "orthodoxy gone cultic" by Fuller Theological Seminary president E. J. Carnell,[18] is not the only alternative to liberal Christianity. Self-identified progressive Christians need to understand that and the serious dangers of liberal theology and discover a contemporary, relevant, biblical, and orthodox middle ground between the two.

---

18. E. J. Carnell, *The Case for Orthodox Theology* (Louisville: Westminster, 1959), 113.

INDEX

Index

God-consciousness (*continued*)
- salvation as increase of, 42, 125, 127, 143
- sin as lack of, 125, 143

Grenz, Stanley J., 172

Harnack, Adolf von, 3, 26–27
Harvey, Van, 51, 168
Hegel, Georg Wilhelm Friedrich, 79, 88, 110
hell
- as alienation from God, 148
- as lack of God-consciousness, 23
- liberal Christian lack of belief in, 13, 23, 124–25, 147–49, 159
- orthodox Christian views on, 23, 154
- as permanence of every fulfillment and destruction, 137, 154–55
- as result of lack of repentance, 131, 141
- and sin, 123, 131, 154
- Unitarian lack of belief in, 12, 13, 141

Hermann, Wilhelm, 5
higher criticism, 56–57, 66, 71
Hodgson, Peter C.
- and authoritative norms of liberal theology, 49
- and eschatology, 156–57
- and God, 88, 156–57
- and the Holy Spirit, 89
- influence of, 31
- and Jesus, 110–11, 156–57
- and salvation, 138–39
- and the Trinity, 89

Hume, David, 76, 77
Hutchison, William R.
- criticism of liberal theology, 170
- and freedom, 128–29
- and God, 32, 80, 97
- influence of, 32–33
- works of on liberal Christianity, 4, 31, 32

hypostatic union, 119

immanence of God
- liberal view of, 32, 52, 79, 80–81, 86, 90, 137
- orthodox view of, 32, 77
immortality
- objective, 147, 155, 158, 160
- of the soul, 149
- subjective, 147, 152, 158, 160
Irenaeus, 13

Jesus Christ
- atoning death of. *See* atonement
- divinity of. *See* divinity of Jesus
- as eternal God, 35, 72, 100, 115
- as fully God-conscious, 116, 125, 127, 128
- as the God-filled man, 21
- heresies concerning, 100–101
- incarnation of. *See* divinity of Jesus
- liberal Christian view of, 99–120
- and the millennium, 145–46
- Mormon view of, 35, 35n. 1
- as perfection of human personality, 32
- process theology view of, 31
- resurrection of. *See* resurrection of Jesus
- return of. *See* parousia, the
- Ritschl's view of, 25–26
- and salvation, 121, 122–23, 130, 131, 133, 143
- Schleiermacher's view of, 20, 76
- Tillich's view of, 30
- virgin birth of, 46, 70, 72, 85
- worship of, 108

Jesus Seminar, the, 71

Kant, Immanuel, 7, 25, 151
Kaufman, Gordon, 93
King, Henry Churchill
- and authoritative norms of liberal theology, 43–44
- and the Bible, 66–67
- criticism of liberal theology, 170
- and eschatology, 151
- and God, 82, 83–84
- and Jesus, 28, 105
- and the kingdom of God, 151
- and law, 83–84
- as mediating theologian, 67, 82
- and miracles, 82, 83
- and salvation, 131, 132
- and sin, 131, 132
- works of, 28

kingdom of God, the, 25, 26, 27, 29, 103, 148, 166

Lewis, C. S., 38, 77, 100
liberal Christianity
- adherents to, 172–73
- authority for belief of, 7–9, 35–52, 56, 59, 61–62
- and authority of Scripture, 8, 23, 25, 31, 35–52, 55–73

liberal Christianity (*continued*)
  and authority of the self, 22
  crisis of, 163–74
  decline in numbers and influence of,
    163–64, 165, 166, 174
  definition of, 1, 6–7, 8–9, 173–74
  diversity of, 2
  and divinity of Jesus, 11, 23, 28, 49,
    99–120
  and God, 23, 32, 49, 52, 75–97
  and hell, 23, 124
  and higher criticism, 56, 57
  history of, 12, 25–28, 33
  and immanence of God, 32, 52, 79,
    80–81, 86, 90, 137
  and the kingdom of God, 25, 26, 27,
    29, 103, 166
  liberal Christian criticism of, 167–68,
    170–72
  and liberation from oppression, 63
  loss of optimism of, 166
  and miracles, 23, 32, 42, 58, 64, 75, 77
  as not authentically Christian, 4–6,
    11, 14, 41, 73, 144, 147, 161, 164–65
  origins of, 2, 3, 12–13
  orthodox Christian criticism of,
    164–65
  and prayer, 58
  vs. progressive Christianity, 1–2,
    173–74
  prototypes of, 18–22, 25–28, 31
  and reducing religion to ethics, 25,
    26, 27
  and the resurrection of Christ, 23–24,
    30, 31, 42, 46, 76, 115
  and salvation, 23, 42, 121–44
  and sin, 52, 96, 101, 125, 129–31,
    136–37, 143
  sources and norms of, 35–52
  and the Trinity, 13, 20, 21, 23, 52, 85,
    89, 94
  and universal salvation, 23, 124,
    135–36, 142, 147, 149
  and wrath of God, 91, 96, 97, 124, 131
liberal theology. *See* liberal
  Christianity
liberation from oppression, 63, 138–39
Lindbeck, George, 94–95
Lippmann, Walter, 5

Machen, J. Gresham, 5, 33, 164–65
McKnight, Scot, 172

Miller, Donald E.
  and authoritative norms of liberal
    theology, 45–47
  and the Bible, 69, 70, 72
  criticism of liberal theology, 171
  and eschatology, 156
  and God, 87–88
  influence of, 31
  and Jesus, 69, 70–71, 109
  and miracles, 46, 70–71
  and salvation, 138
  and symbolic realism, 70, 138
miracles
  higher criticism and, 57
  liberal Christian lack of belief in, 23,
    32, 42, 58, 64, 75, 77
  modernity and, 7, 24
  orthodox Christian belief in, 23, 76, 77
  process theology view of, 31
  and science, 24, 78
  as symbolic, 24
  as symbols of spiritual
    transformation, 64
modalism, 94
modernity, 6–7, 59, 61
monism, 80
moralizing of dogma, 132, 133

naturalism, 30, 38
Nicene Creed, the, 14
Niebuhr, H. Richard, 96, 147, 159, 166

Oden, Thomas, 171–72
orthodox Christianity
  and authority of the Bible, 8, 23, 36,
    38–39, 53–55, 73
  and divinity of Jesus, 11, 23, 38, 49
  and immanence of God, 32, 77
  and the kingdom of God, 148
  and liberation from oppression, 63
  and miracles, 23, 76, 77
  normative beliefs of, 23, 38
  and the resurrection of Jesus, 23, 38,
    62–63, 122
  and salvation, 23, 38, 121–23, 131, 139
  and science, 37–38, 46
  and sin, 91, 121, 123, 141, 153
  and symbolism, 24–25
  and transcendence of God, 32, 52, 75,
    77, 79, 80, 90
  and the Trinity, 23, 38, 76, 105, 119
  view of God, 23, 52, 75–77, 84, 89, 90